When the Shooting Stopped

When the Shooting Stopped

Crisis Negotiations at Jefferson High School

Laurie L. Charlés

ROWMAN & LITTLEFIELD PUBLISHERS, INC.
Lanham • Boulder • New York • Toronto • Plymouth, UK

ROWMAN & LITTLEFIELD PUBLISHERS, INC.

Published in the United States of America
by Rowman & Littlefield Publishers, Inc.
A wholly owned subsidiary of The Rowman & Littlefield Publishing Group, Inc.
4501 Forbes Boulevard, Suite 200, Lanham, Maryland 20706
www.rowmanlittlefield.com

Estover Road
Plymouth PL6 7PY
United Kingdom

Copyright © 2008 by Rowman & Littlefield Publishers, Inc.

All rights reserved. No part of this publication may be reproduced, stored in a retrieval system, or transmitted in any form or by any means, electronic, mechanical, photocopying, recording, or otherwise, without the prior permission of the publisher.

British Library Cataloguing in Publication Information Available

Library of Congress Cataloging-in-Publication Data

Charlés, Laurie L.
 When the shooting stopped : crisis negotiation at Jefferson High School / Laurie L. Charlés.
   p. cm.
 Includes bibliographical references.
 ISBN-13: 978-0-7425-6087-1 (cloth : alk. paper)
 ISBN-10: 0-7425-6087-2 (cloth : alk. paper)
 ISBN-13: 978-0-7425-6088-8 (pbk. : alk. paper)
 ISBN-10: 0-7425-6088-0 (pbk. : alk. paper)
  1. Hostage negotiations—United States—Case studies. 2. Communication in law enforcement—United States—Case studies. 3. School shootings—United States—Case studies. I. Title.

HV8058.C33 2008
363.2'32—dc22
2007035977

Printed in the United States of America

∞™ The paper used in this publication meets the minimum requirements of American National Standard for Information Sciences—Permanence of Paper for Printed Library Materials, ANSI/NISO Z39.48-1992.

Contents

Acknowledgments		vii
Introduction		1
1	A Brief History of Crisis Negotiation	7
2	Method of Inquiry and Approach to the Analysis	11
3	The 1st Moment: 4:25 P.M.	33
4	The 2nd Moment: 6:00 P.M.	59
5	The 3rd Moment: 6:15 P.M.	67
6	The 4th Moment: 8:30 P.M.	87
7	The 5th Moment: 9:40 P.M.	97
8	Nine Techniques of Effective Crisis Negotiation	105
9	Implications of the Study	123
References		129
Index		133
About the Author		141

Acknowledgments

A book, particularly one that is a qualitative research inquiry, is inherently a product shaped by many people. I am fortunate to have had a large "supporting cast" of family, friends, and colleagues that supported me throughout the three years of this research. Dr. Douglas Flemons, Dr. Shelley Green, Dr. Ron Chenail, and Dr. Chris Burnett, all faculty members in the Family Therapy program at Nova Southeastern University, provided tremendous expertise, enthusiasm, and vision, which sustained me throughout the project and continues to inform my work to this day. The numerous crisis negotiation researchers, academics, and practitioners who I met at the FBI Academy and in police departments throughout the country provided endless stories, suggestions, and commentary that both complemented and inspired my research interest in the topic. I remain deeply indebted to the Jefferson negotiators for their contribution to this inquiry. The research came "alive" when I involved them in it; it has been my goal ever since to construct a final product that does justice to their work.

Introduction

PRELUDE TO A HOSTAGE CRISIS

The young man had experienced many bad days lately, and this one was no different. His plans were the same: target practice out in the desert. He didn't want anyone to know he'd lost his job and was no longer at work during the day. But instead of driving to his usual spot, he found himself driving down the lane leading to the high school. He didn't expect to be here today, but here he was. He had known the moment would come. He just hadn't known when.

He stopped his car in front of the Arts Building at Jefferson High School[1] and arranged his gear: candy bars, shells, and his gun. Ms. Munroe, the drama teacher, saw him. She thought it was odd that he was wearing army fatigues and had a gun slung over his shoulder. But then she remembered that the civics classes were studying riot behavior, and she assumed that he was part of some group demonstration. She did not give him another thought until much later.

He did not see her. He was walking straight to Room 202—his old teacher Mr. Grant's room. Grant had flunked him five years earlier. As a result, he did not graduate, and later he lost his job when they found out he did not have a diploma. Worse, he had missed his prom, and then he and his girlfriend broke up. He was still pissed off about it. As he approached the door, he could hear Mr. Grant, talking about compound sentences. Grant saw him too late. The young man raised his gun and with perfect aim shot Grant in the chest. Grant died instantly. The youth looked around the room. It was so quiet. The students stared up at him, dumbfounded. Finally one girl got up out of her desk and screamed. The man shot her and walked out of the room.

1

He started toward the back door of the building, but soon found himself surrounded by students. They were running and screaming and falling over each other. One girl came very close and this discomfited him. Looking right at her, he raised his gun once again, but unexpectedly a boy got between them. He shot the boy instead. Then he heard the sirens. Shit. He ran upstairs to the library. There were at least a hundred kids up here. Fine. He didn't know what he'd do with them, but he wasn't leaving now.

The first police officers to arrive at the scene quickly realized they had a serious incident on their hands: mortally wounded students and teachers, an unknown shooter, and hostages. The department, small and in a rural area, had never seen anything like it. A call for aid was placed to a neighboring police department and the closest FBI field office. In the meantime, the police hoped that they could convince the shooter to come out of the building peacefully. Several officers had already been inside the Arts Building and gone as far as the staircase. To their surprise, they had made contact with the young man, who had stopped shooting and agreed to talk, but only over the phone. Excellent. They would start with that.

CASE STUDY OF A CRISIS NEGOTIATION

Hostage incidents at schools are tragic, recurring phenomena in the United States. Each incident is unique in its demographics; however, one defining feature of all life-threatening critical incidents is that a group of law enforcement professionals will be called to manage the crisis *as it is unfolding*. These professionals must be flexible in their approach and tailor their work according to what they find at the scene. Tragically, as in the recent incident at Virginia Polytechnic University in Blacksburg, sometimes all that is left to find at the scene is death and destruction. In some cases, however, police may arrive at the scene in a position to *prevent* the death and destruction. Crisis management in critical incidents requires more than skill at sharpshooting; in the case of hostage situations, it may require conversational expertise.

What happens at the moment in which the opportunity for meaningful conversation occurs? How is it possible to elicit change, through dialogue, during a life-threatening situation? This book illustrates how a team of seven crisis negotiators—law enforcement officers with specialized training in crisis intervention—established a meaningful dialogue with the young man described above. In the midst of a tense situation with additional lives on the line, these negotiators skillfully used conversation to bring this deadly incident to a peaceful conclusion. The conversational approach these negotiators took, and the role they established as patient, interested, and curious listeners, literally disarmed him.[2]

In the following chapters, I will discuss my research on the crisis negotiation that took place following the events described above. How did police establish meaningful dialogue with someone who did not want to talk to them? How did they use language to establish rapport with someone who had already shot numerous people? How did they monitor their efforts throughout the eight-hour incident?

This study is an in-depth analysis of one crisis negotiation discursive event. I relied on qualitative research methods that helped me examine the event in a way that was comprehensive, credible, and expansive. I took the position that it is crisis negotiation practitioners who are true experts on the highly complex crisis negotiation process; in particular, the negotiators present at each incident have a great deal of expertise to share about the discourse process at that incident. Their thoughts, ideas, and views about the different features of the discourse were necessary for the type of inquiry I wanted to conduct.

In addition to including the views and ideas of the Jefferson crisis negotiators, I also incorporated an expert in the field of crisis negotiation, Gary Noesner, former chief of the Crisis Negotiation Unit at the Federal Bureau of Investigation's (FBI) Training Academy in Quantico, Virginia.[3] Noesner was not present at the Jefferson incident, but he is widely published and well known for his practice, instruction, and advocacy of the conversational skills needed in effective crisis management.

This study is an examination of a successful crisis negotiation, a typical, ordinary, "good job." It also is unique in that it illustrates an in-depth examination of the work of crisis negotiation by incorporating the incident negotiators' points of view on their discourse process. There is a lack of research on crisis negotiation that incorporates the views, perspectives, and knowledge of practitioners in the research process. Thus, this research project addresses a major gap in the field of crisis negotiation research.

The Jefferson crisis negotiation demonstrates how a team of negotiators worked together to construct a powerful discourse effort that resulted in a hostage taker's surrender. Their effort prevented further loss of life. The goal of my study was to take a clinical perspective toward examination of how the negotiators achieved a successful end to the incident through their use of discourse. Their work practices have tremendous implications for law enforcement professionals at every level—including the ones who will be called upon to resolve crises that occur in the communities in which we live.

My microanalysis of the discourse, using the views of the negotiators as a lens to understand the talk, elicited a very powerful description of how the shooting stopped at Jefferson High School. The methods I used and the manner in which I illustrate the discourse complexity outlines how conversational techniques transformed the outcome of the hostage incident negotiators were faced with when they arrived at the scene.

OVERVIEW OF THE JEFFERSON INCIDENT

The incident at Jefferson High School lasted approximately eight hours. The shooting occurred in the early afternoon, about 2:10 P.M., and actual taped discourse with the hostage taker began about 4:20 P.M., lasting until 10:20 P.M. The negotiation that took place in those hours was actually a series of conversations. Many of these were between negotiator Paul and a hostage named Alan. Alan often had to act as interpreter between Paul and the hostage taker. His early interpretations were a source of difficulty for the team, and one of their first tasks was to develop a productive working relationship with him.

Alan had to speak for the team because the hostage taker often refrained from discussion with Paul. The hostage taker, who in the first phone call identified himself as Leo, regularly avoided the telephone. He was busy watching for snipers and attending to the large group of hostages. Leo's hesitancy had a discernible pattern; each time he participated in a discussion with Paul, he tended to avoid the next series of calls. Dealing with Leo's refusal to come to the phone became another important task for the negotiators.

The substantive conversations in the negotiation were about the following issues: Leo had recently lost his job (because he did not have a diploma) and his girlfriend; he related these losses to flunking school; and he blamed his former teacher Mr. Grant for the disappointments this caused in his life. Many other conversations occurred around less personal, but not less important, issues, such as ordering pizza and soda for the students and Leo's repeated requests to view a television and speak to a reporter. Negotiators did not give Leo access to a television or a reporter; however, Leo located a radio and heard late in the incident that one of the people he had shot was dead and others were hospitalized.

The last part of the negotiation involved discussion about the prison sentence Leo would face for what he had done. Leo and Paul made a specific agreement about Leo's sentence, his prison cell, and potential educational opportunities while in prison. The agreement was a ritual of surrender; it came in the form of a letter from the team. Leo accepted the letter believing he had not killed anyone. Despite the radio report to the contrary, Paul convinced Leo that no one had died. At the time he surrendered, Leo appeared not to know that he had killed four people.

OVERVIEW OF THE BOOK

Crisis negotiation refers to the dialogical effort undertaken by specially trained law enforcement officers during police critical incidents. In the first chapter, I will discuss the basic elements of crisis negotiation practice and the history of the field. While I do not intend this book to be a "how-to" text on crisis negotiation, nor a treatise on the political ramifications of the process, the story within its pages is a "textbook example"—as one negotiator called it—of a successfully resolved incident. In this case, the shooting stopped because of the dialogical effort of law enforcement officers at the scene. That effort is what I focus on in this book.

The history of the field of crisis negotiation in chapter 1 sets a context for the study of the Jefferson incident. In chapter 2, I discuss the method of inquiry I chose to study the Jefferson High School negotiation and the approach I took to analyzing and interpreting the discourse that occurred between negotiators and the hostage taker in this confrontation.

The Jefferson incident lasted more than eight hours, the dialogue for nearly four. During those four hours, five key moments of change occurred in the conversation between hostage taker and negotiators—at 4:25 P.M., 6:00 P.M., 6:15 P.M., 8:30 P.M., and 9:40 P.M. Those five moments are examined individually in chapters 3 through 7, displaying the verbatim dialogue and including the comments and interpretations of the team members in the analysis of the talk. In chapter 8, I summarize the nine techniques of effective crisis negotiation used by the Jefferson team, and in chapter 9, I discuss the implications of the study.

In contemporary American society, hostage situations—particularly in our schools—continue to be a tragic reality. In-depth, qualitative examination of the discourse events that occur during such life-threatening hostage incidents contributes valuable information toward our understanding of how to defuse these violent situations. In addition, a focused case study such as the one detailed in this book tells us something about the often hidden efforts of crisis negotiators—the behind-the-scenes work that goes into constructing lifesaving discourse.

This study illustrates vividly what worked in one incident, and it provides valuable clues about what can work in other crises like it. Numerous inferences can be drawn from the story of law enforcement negotiators at Jefferson High School. First, however, it is necessary to understand the history of crisis negotiation, to which I turn my attention in chapter 1.

NOTES

1. I have changed the name of the high school.
2. I thank Muriel Singer for first capturing for me the idea that crisis negotiators "disarm" people with words.
3. His name is used with permission.

Chapter One

A Brief History of Crisis Negotiation

Police officers are the first professionals who respond to and become involved in a variety of conflicts between people (Bolz, 1981; Everstine, Bodin, & Everstine, 1977), some of whom may be in the midst of a psychological or emotional crisis (Fuselier, 1988). When these crises become life threatening, as in the case of hostage taking or a suicide attempt, police have two options: they can end the incident with force, in an assault/rescue attempt (Friedland & Merari, 1992; Fuselier, 1981a; Goldaber, 1979; Heyman, 1993), or they can try to end it peacefully through a conversation with the person. If police choose the latter option, they enlist crisis negotiators—law enforcement officers trained in crisis intervention.

Crisis negotiation is the law enforcement practice of talking to hostage takers and other barricaded individuals. A difficult, emotional, stressful, and dangerous process (Dalfonzo & Romano, 2003; Terhune-Bickler, 2004), this endeavor has been traditionally known as *hostage negotiation*. However, the term *crisis negotiation* is considered a more apt description of the activity, and it more accurately reflects the kind of situations law enforcement officers deal with on a regular basis (Rogan & Hammer, 1994).

Law enforcement agencies developed hostage negotiation techniques after a number of terrorist events in the early 1970s (Danto, 1979; Gist & Perry, 1985) and numerous hostage incidents during the same period (Feldmann & Johnson, 1995; Rodriguez & Franklin, 1986). Prior to 1972, hostage standoffs were handled in one way: police officers demanded the person surrender, and if that failed, they ended the incident with combative tactics, including crossfire and eventual assault (Donohue, Ramesh, Kaufmann, & Smith, 1991; Maher, 1977; McMains & Mullins, 1996). This approach tended to result in deaths and injury, sometimes to the very people police were trying to help (Aston, 1983; Miller, 1979).

Dr. Harvey Schlossberg, a trained psychologist who worked with the New York Police Department in the 1970s, is credited with formulating the first model of hostage negotiation. He recommended that police take a crisis intervention approach (McMains & Mullins, 1996; Schlossberg, 1979) and advocated three basic negotiation strategies:

1. Take as much time as needed to resolve an incident.
2. Focus on establishing and maintaining a conversation with the person.
3. Limit the involvement of others at the scene.

Schlossberg trained hundreds of police officers and captains in the negotiation techniques he advocated, and soon hostage negotiation became standard training in all New York precincts, in other police departments in the state (Schlossberg & Freeman, 1974), and eventually at the FBI.

The success of the NYPD hostage negotiation unit and the establishment of a similar unit at the FBI lent credibility and legitimacy to the hostage negotiation process (McMains & Mullins, 1996). However, these techniques remained a voluntary police effort; there was no legal precedent requiring police to use them. That changed with a court decision in 1975, based on an incident that established hostage negotiation as a legal mandate (McMains & Mullins, 1996).

Interestingly, hostages are not necessary for a hostage negotiation to take place (Maher, 1977), and hostage incidents are not the primary type of crisis with which law enforcement agencies deal (McMains & Mullins, 1996; Regini, 2002). Rather, police officers most often negotiate with a person who is in the midst of an escalated personal crisis:

> The majority of critical incidents to which law enforcement responds involve subjects who are motivated primarily by emotional needs . . . [and] these incidents may involve jilted lovers, disgruntled employees, or students, mood-disordered or psychotic subjects, suicidal individuals, or individuals, who, for whatever reason, believe that they or their beliefs have been threatened or demeaned by society. (Noesner & Webster, 1997, p. 13)

The incidents to which crisis negotiators primarily respond are suicide attempts, domestic disputes, and hostage takings (Hammer, Van Zandt, & Rogan, 1994; Kraus, Wilkenfeld, Harris, & Blake, 1992; Wind, 1995). Regini (2004) noted that "the overwhelming majority of hostage-barricade incidents handled by police negotiators are nonhostage" (p. 2).

To deal with these incidents, police departments tend to select negotiators on the basis of their knowledge, as well as certain personal qualities (Welch, 1984).

These include basic common sense (Maher, 1977); a cool, resourceful, and mature personality (Culley, 1974); and an ability to accept "abuse, ridicule, and insults" (Fuselier, 1981b). Furthermore, Bolz (1981) recommended that negotiators have "lay psychological experience," Regini (2002) that they have "some knowledge of behavioral sciences," and Fuselier (1981b) that they be committed to the process. In addition, negotiators must be able to think clearly, listen well, have excellent interviewing skills, and be streetwise (Fuselier, 1981b).

Regini (2002) also pointed out that

> the best criminal investigators tend to be the best crisis negotiators. Strong criminal investigators will have had contact with a wide variety of people in diverse, and often stressful and dangerous, circumstances. Further, the nonconfrontational and nonjudgmental approach of a good negotiator typically is found in criminal investigators who possess exceptional interview and interrogation skills. (p. 2)

A crisis negotiator has to learn to establish a relationship with hostage takers in spite of their police instincts (Donohue & Roberto, 1993; Ramesh, 1992, as cited in Donohue & Roberto, 1993, p. 196; Soskis, 1983). According to McMains and Mullins (1996), officers must undergo a paradigm shift in order to become effective crisis negotiators:

> The negotiators know they are talking to a person who may kill people. The negotiator is faced with role ambiguity. He is expected to uphold the law, arrest criminals, and protect the public. As a negotiator, he is expected to be able to talk with and become friendly with a criminal. He must set aside his values and beliefs and operate from a different belief structure. (p. 131)

The negotiator not only has to think differently about this relationship but also has to convince the hostage taker that the relationship is different. This is no easy task. People in a standoff with police are highly emotionally aroused, insecure about their safety, fearful of police, and anxious about the entire situation (Donohue et al., 1991; Donohue & Ramesh, 1992; Johnson, 1978). Developing a relationship with a hostage taker is a negotiation in itself (Donohue & Roberto, 1993).

Negotiators try to address the hostage taker's perception of the negotiation process immediately: "As long as the subject perceives the atmosphere as threatening, no meaningful communication can take place" (Noesner & Webster, 1997, p. 16). In order to set the stage for meaningful conversation, the negotiator must first demonstrate a genuine desire to help:

> Negotiators generally achieve peaceful resolutions only after they demonstrate their desire to be nonjudgmental, nonthreatening, and understanding of the subject's feelings. By projecting that understanding, negotiators show empathy and

lead the subject to perceive them, not as the enemy, but as concerned individuals who want to help. (Noesner & Webster, 1997, p. 16)

Negotiators express an interest in understanding the incident from the hostage taker's perspective. They refrain from making value judgments about the hostage taker's behavior (Biggs, 1987; Hassel, 1975; McMains & Mullins, 1996), and they do not challenge or reject the hostage taker outright (Donohue, Ramesh, & Borchgrevink, 1991). The stance negotiators take helps them generate ideas that will be acceptable to the hostage taker (McMains & Mullins, 1996). It also increases trust, strengthens the relationship, and allows the hostage taker to ventilate feelings (Donohue, et al., 1991).

Gaining the hostage taker's trust is essential to the process and is one of the most significant issues facing the negotiator (Donohue, Ramesh, & Borchgrevink, 1991; Donohue, et al., 1991). Instead of "intimidating, demeaning, lecturing, criticizing, and evaluating" (Noesner & Webster, 1997, p. 16), a negotiator asks open-ended questions, such as, "Can you tell me what happened here today?" These questions allow the hostage taker to express views and talk as much as possible (DiVasto, Lanceley, & Gruys, 1992; Fuselier, 1981b).

Crisis negotiators listen for "hooks," topic areas that promote "conversation, self-disclosure, and, ultimately, bonding" (DiVasto & Newman, 1993; Slatkin, 2003). Hooks have also been defined as personal values that are a potential source of theme development during a crisis negotiation (Regini, 2004). Similarly, negotiators are careful to avoid using certain words, such as "surrender," "giving up," or "failing" (Biggs, 1987; Fuselier, 1981b; McMains & Mullins, 1996; Noesner & Dolan, 1992). Furthermore, negotiators have learned the importance of a present-focused, contextually sensitive approach to talking to people in crisis. In order to "lead the subject out of crisis, the negotiator must appreciate the factors that created the situation in the first place" (Noesner & Webster, 1997, p. 14).

The communication skills that negotiators use range from basic communication principles to the application of sophisticated hypnotic suggestion techniques (McMains & Mullins, 1996; Reiser & Sloane, 1983). However, the most significant of the communication skills that negotiators rely on are active listening skills (Noesner & Webster, 1997).

Negotiators have to deal with police officials listening in on the negotiation, media people monitoring the situation, and SWAT officers positioning to shoot the hostage taker. In addition, negotiators are surrounded by paramedics and rescue squads, police commanders and assisting officers, interested bystanders and family members, and reporters from newspaper and television (McMains & Mullins, 1996). As happened in the Jefferson incident, the presence of these other people can directly affect the negotiation process and potentially exacerbate it (Friedland & Merari, 1992).

Chapter Two

Method of Inquiry and Approach to the Analysis

This book focuses on one specific crisis negotiation incident. By focusing exclusively on the talk of one incident, I gained an in-depth understanding of the discourse and also learned something about crisis discourse in general. The in-depth case study approach is in the spirit of Tannen's (1989) suggestion that "the accurate representation of the particular communicates universality, whereas direct attempts to represent universality often communicate nothing" (p. 105).

In this chapter, I outline the methods I chose to use in performing the inquiry. I discuss my research assumptions, my immersion in the field of crisis negotiation, and the fieldwork interviews I conducted at the site of the shooting and in other parts of the country. At the end of the chapter, I describe the credibility of my research methods and explain how I pulled all of the data together to construct a document by which I was able to conduct a formal discourse analysis. In the next section, I will describe the assumptions of qualitative inquiry and discuss how those assumptions informed my research questions and methodology.

∼

The original research question guiding this project was this: What are the patterns of talk in a successful crisis negotiation discourse? Soon after I became immersed in the world of crisis negotiation, however, other questions also presented themselves as relevant: How did a relationship develop between the negotiators and the hostage taker? How did they construct the dialogue? In order to address these questions in a comprehensive way, I highlight the views of crisis negotiation practitioners in this study. Incorporating the outlook of these practitioners compelled me to take a naturalistic approach to the inquiry and use qualitative, inductive methods to gather and generate the data.

The crisis negotiation I focused on in this study is actually a series of many conversations between two people—a police officer and a high school dropout turned hostage taker. The hostage taker entered a school and shot several people before taking a classroom of students hostage. However, shooting ceased once law enforcement officers arrived at the scene, and before long, negotiations began. After approximately eight hours, the hostage taker released his hostages and surrendered. Though the hostage taker spoke primarily to one negotiator during the incident, a team of seven negotiators participated in the process. As I was to soon learn, the other team members provided ideas, feedback, and suggestions to the primary negotiator and were an integral part of the discourse process.

A NATURALISTIC APPROACH TO THE RESEARCH

My research approach to crisis negotiation discourse was informed by the assumptions of naturalistic inquiry (Lincoln & Guba, 1985). In a naturalistic inquiry, the researcher explores meanings and experiences rather than confirming or rejecting a preexisting hypothesis. I wanted to understand how the Jefferson crisis negotiation discourse worked and how negotiators would attribute meaning to their work. My research question was about understanding a *process*—the process of how communication skills were used in a successful crisis negotiation. Thus, it required research methods that are contextual and that elicit descriptive information, such as in-depth interviews, participant observation, and fieldwork.

In order to best understand the patterns in the crisis negotiation in the Jefferson incident, it was necessary for me to think about not only facts or causes but also meaning. In this study, questions about meaning had to focus on the perspective of the participants in the actual dialogue. It is their perspective that my research tried to capture as accurately as possible (Bogdan & Biklen, 1982).

In addition to my curiosity about how negotiators attributed meaning to the discourse, I also focused my attention on an audiotaped discourse that is an official record of a crisis negotiation with a hostage taker. I obtained a copy of this audiotape from negotiators at the FBI Training Academy. It is routine practice for law enforcement officers to record their conversations during hostage-taking or barricade incidents, and the FBI maintains an archive of many of these tapes. I reviewed several before choosing the Jefferson incident to study.

REFINING THE METHOD

Initially, I did not plan to include any interviews with negotiators in my examination of the Jefferson discourse. However, I happened to meet one of the Jefferson negotiators, Patricia,[1] during my yearlong immersion into the world of crisis negotiation. During "hospitality hour" at a law enforcement conference, Patricia and I chatted about my study and her participation at the incident. When I complimented the work of the primary negotiator, Paul, Patricia interrupted me abruptly. She told me that the Jefferson negotiation had been a team effort, not the work of one person: "Do you remember when the hostage taker said he would release ten people and the negotiator said release twenty-five and he did? That was me who suggested that. I thought, hey, if he'll release ten, why not fifteen? Or twenty? Or twenty-five? So we got him to release twenty-five."

From my repeated listenings and my transcription of the Jefferson tape, I knew that this passage of dialogue seemed to be a pivotal point in the negotiation. However, there was no indication on the tape itself that a team member had contributed the remark. Patricia revealed other important details as well: she described how the team conducted the negotiation in a tiny room near the school's main office, explained that most of them wore headphones to listen to the dialogue, stated that they were all present throughout the incident, and described how each had played an active part in the negotiation.

After meeting Patricia and thinking more about what I had learned (and could learn) from her, I made an important decision: I would contact and interview all of the law enforcement officers who had played a role in the Jefferson negotiation discourse. Interviews with the Jefferson team would give me an insider's perspective of the negotiation. In qualitative inquiry, such understanding is essential in order to accurately describe the phenomenon under study (Fetterman, 1989).

At first, I thought that a focus group interview would be the best way to incorporate negotiators into the research process. However, upon contacting the Jefferson negotiators, several things became clear. I had assumed that the negotiators knew each other and worked together both before and after the incident. When I spoke to them, however, I learned that they actually did not know each other prior to the incident, nor had they worked together as a group since then. In fact, with a few exceptions, they had not seen each other since the Jefferson incident. This was something I did not expect—they had worked so well together on tape that I took for granted they had had an excellent pre- and postincident working relationship. I was wrong.

While each team member explained that they had had an excellent working relationship during the incident, some said that after it was over, their relationships had become tense and distant. In the words of one team member, they had "gone to shit." Although some team members had remained close and were agreeable to a group interview, others expressed wariness and rejected the idea.

Taylor and Bogdan (1984) noted that "the preconceived image we have of the people we intend to study may be naive, misleading, or downright false" (p. 16). In the Jefferson case, the real-life relationships between participants illustrated how little sense it made to pursue a group interview. I decided to interview the team in dyads or triads. However, this soon proved logistically difficult: team members lived in three different communities and some had retired, changed jobs, or planned vacations during the time of my visit. In the end, I held all of the interviews individually.

I further refined my interview protocol as a result of these introductory conversations. Initially, I had planned to interview the team members solely about the discourse. I underestimated their personal desire and professional interest in talking about the Jefferson incident. Most had not had the opportunity to discuss the incident with anyone (certainly not a researcher), and each was eager to talk about it. This was a surprise I welcomed; I was fascinated listening to the stories of these negotiators.

I made one more significant change to the interview protocol after my initial face-to-face contact with the participants. I realized that just one interview with participants was insufficient. The Jefferson negotiators wanted to talk about more than the negotiation process; they also wanted to discuss the overall critical incident. Thus, I conducted several interviews with the negotiators, which were inclusive of their experience of the incident as well the specifics of the discourse process. In qualitative research interviewing, it is difficult to know how many interviews to conduct with participants until the researcher actually begins speaking to participants face-to-face (Taylor & Bogdan, 1984).

COMBINING METHODS THAT APPRECIATE CONTEXT: DISCOURSE ANALYSIS, ETHNOGRAPHY, AND IPR

This study combined methods of discourse analysis, ethnography, and Interpersonal Process Recall (IPR) in order to make sense of the data in a comprehensive way. In combination, these methods more fully captured the complexity of the Jefferson crisis negotiation. They allowed a way for me to comprehend, synthesize, and recontextualize (Morse, 1994) the data and were consistent with an inductive inquiry. This methodology also helped increase a research understanding of the data in a systematic way (Bogdan & Biklen, 1982).

Discourse Analysis

Discourse analysis was a way to examine how the negotiators used language during the course of their interaction with the hostage taker (Potter & Wetherell, 1987). By looking closely at the negotiation talk and its organization, as well as considering the context of the discourse (Potter & Wetherell, 1987), I began to make sense of it as a constructed process.

In a discourse analysis, descriptions of the talk will vary from participant to participant, depending on that person's perceptions of the function and purpose of the talk (Potter & Wetherell, 1987, p. 33). In this study, I found that each of the participants viewed the discourse differently, according to their perceptions of, experiences with, and assumptions about crisis negotiation. In incorporating their different views, it was possible to obtain a more comprehensive understanding of the discourse (Potter & Wetherell, 1987).

Discourse Analysis and Ethnographic Interviewing

In this study, I took Moerman's (1988) suggestion and combined my discourse analysis with ethnography. Moerman (1988) advocated that a discourse analysis be combined with an ethnographic approach because conversations are not merely discourse events—they are human events. Studying a conversation independently of the setting in which it occurred is faulty, according to Moerman, because ignoring the context and the purpose of a conversation distorts the attempt to describe it. In Moerman's (1988) view, analysis of a conversation "require[s] a synthesis of ethnography—with its concern for context, meaning, history, and intention" (p. xi). Ethnography requires fieldwork (Fetterman, 1989) and can include various forms of interviewing and participant observation.

Ethnographic Interview Process

I conducted ethnographic interviews with all team members. Ethnographic interviews are open-ended, unstructured, and "sacrifice uniformity of questioning to achieve fuller development of information" (Weiss, 1994, p. 3). They require a particular type of research stance—one that demonstrates curiosity and genuine interest and is devoid of preexisting hypotheses or assumptions:

> Ethnographers adopt a particular stance toward people with whom they work. By word and by action, in subtle ways and direct statements, they say, "I want to understand the world from your point of view. I want to know what you know in the way you know it. I want to understand the meaning of your experience,

to walk in your shoes, to feel things as you feel them, to explain things as you explain them." (Spradley, 1979, p. 34)

Ethnographic interviews provided a way for participants to talk about their experience of the Jefferson negotiation in their own words (Taylor & Bogdan, 1984). For me, the Jefferson participants were a conduit to learn about what happened in an event that exists in the past. They acted as observers and informants about the crisis negotiation that took place (Taylor & Bogdan, 1984).

In order to conduct the interviews, I spent seven days in the community where the Jefferson incident took place. Of course, it was not possible to observe the Jefferson participants "at work" during the incident itself. However, it was indeed possible to learn about their experience of this past event through in-depth interviews with them. Taylor and Bogdan (1984) addressed the role of in-depth interviews toward understanding an event that cannot be directly observed:

> In this type of interviewing the people being interviewed are informants in the truest sense of the word. They act as the researcher's observer, his or her eyes and ears in the field. As informants, their role is not simply to reveal their own views, but to describe what happened and how others viewed it. (p. 78–79)

Furthermore, the interviews had a retrospective nature to them. They centered on an incident that took place several years ago. While retrospective interviews do not always elicit accurate data, they are the only way to gather information about past events:

> In situations where the ethnographer already has an accurate understanding of the historical facts, a retrospective interview provides useful information about the individual. The manner in which individuals shape the past highlights their values and reveals the configuration of their worldview. (Fetterman, 1989, p. 50)

Spradley (1979) outlined several kinds of useful ethnographic questions, many of which I used during the interviews with negotiators. These ethnographic questions included such categories as:

- grand tour questions ("Can you tell me about your experience as a crisis negotiator in this incident?")
- typical-day questions ("Can you walk me through a typical negotiation incident?")
- guided questions ("Can you tell me what it was like when you arrived at the scene?")

- task-related questions ("Can you draw me a map of what the negotiation room looked like? Who sat where?")

By the end of my research trip to the Jefferson area, I had collected thirty-seven hours of audiotaped interviews with participants. These interviews took place over fourteen separate meetings with the team members. In a later section, I will elaborate further on the individual interviews with each Jefferson participant.

Interpersonal Process Recall

The IPR interviews with participants generated significant and rich data about their experience of the discourse. IPR is a unique interview method that has been used as a training tool for counselors, as a research method for studying psychotherapy process (Elliot, 1986; Kagan & Kagan, 1990), and with couples in marital therapy (Gale, Odell, & Nagireddy, 1995). The hallmark of the IPR interview method is that it provides an opportunity for participants to reflect on their conversation by using an actual recording of that conversation.

During an IPR interview, a "conversation is taped and immediately played back for the participants" (Elliot, 1986, p. 503). Listening to the taped conversation gives IPR participants a direct and vivid way to explore their experience of it. As the IPR participant listens to the audio playback, he or she can "recapture fleeting impressions and reactions which would ordinarily be forgotten or merged into more global perceptions" (Elliott, 1986, p. 503).

An IPR interview procedure cues the memory of participants, allows time for them to find the words to describe their experience, and is direct, specific, and permissive (Elliott, 1986). In IPR, participants control the audio playback of the tape and can stop and start it at any point in order to comment about, reflect on, or clarify something. The entire IPR audio playback process is recorded as data.

To conduct the IPR interviews in this study, I used an audiotaped compilation of excerpts from the Jefferson negotiation. I consulted the Jefferson team prior to making the compilation recording, asking them what parts of the dialogue they particularly remembered and also to identify the exchanges they deemed most significant to the incident's success. I created the tape using their ideas and my own impressions of what had seemed pivotal moments in the eight-hour discourse — and ended up with a collection of five unique moments in the talk. These five excerpts, when recorded together in chronological order, resulted in a tape thirty minutes in length. I used this same compilation tape in all of my interviews with negotiators.

PREPARING FOR DATA COLLECTION

Confidentiality Issues

Hostage incidents tend to be very public events—they are well documented by both law enforcement officials and the media; sometimes only a few details of an incident are sufficient to identify it. In this study, I took many steps to maintain the confidentiality of participants. I renamed the location where the incident took place as Jefferson High School. I also changed the names of the Jefferson negotiators, the hostage taker, the pseudonym the hostage taker used during the incident, and the names of locations relevant to the hostage taking. A primary reason for attending so rigorously to the issue of confidentiality around the identity of the incident was to protect the identity of the hostage taker, as the Jefferson incident continues to be a legal matter for him.

Sampling of the Crisis Negotiation Discourse

I chose to study the Jefferson incident after I had carefully examined six different crisis negotiation audiotapes. These tapes were graphic, compelling, and intense. However, some of tapes were difficult to understand, and others did not seem to have a clear progression—making it impossible to determine how the incident ended. Examining these tapes resulted in a sharper research question. My inquiry focus began to center on the talk of an incident that had ended successfully (i.e., with the hostage taker's surrender) and reflected a progression of how the negotiation unfolded effectively. I also realized that it was necessary to study a tape that was in good condition (a clear recording), understandable, and easy to follow. After these criteria were identified, Gary Noesner produced two potential incident tapes for me to consider. One of these was of the Jefferson incident.

Immersion in the Field of Crisis Negotiation

During the sampling process, but prior to transcribing the tape, contacting the team, or conducting the interviews, I immersed myself in the field of crisis negotiation. I spoke at length to crisis negotiation practitioners and researchers from throughout the United States. One negotiator I met had attended a conference presentation on the Jefferson incident; he gave me a handout from that seminar—a narrative log that detailed certain events during the negotiation. The narrative included comments that reflected some of the team's ideas as they spoke to the hostage taker.

Another negotiator I met gave me a tour of the FBI field office where he worked, and over lunch he talked to me about his experiences in the field. He referred me to crisis negotiators at the FBI Academy; one of them sent me instructional videotapes on crisis negotiation. Several times I phoned authors of articles I thought were especially useful; in turn, they referred me to other negotiators they knew or thought I should talk to. I spoke to two different authors of notable books on crisis negotiation; one was a police negotiator, the other a researcher. Three people I spoke to separately recommended Noesner as an important resource. I was grateful that I was already in contact with him.

Sometimes negotiators referred me to films; one negotiator suggested I watch the movie *Dog Day Afternoon* (which I had never seen) twice—once for entertainment value and once from a researcher's perspective. I also read popular and academic literature on the FBI and crisis negotiation, watched television movies and documentaries about it, and even subscribed to the *FBI Law Enforcement Bulletin*, an important journal in the field of crisis negotiation.

My immersion in the field culminated with my attendance at a three-day crisis negotiation conference in the southeastern United States. Gary Noesner invited me to attend so that I could hear him present as well as meet Patricia, the Jefferson team negotiator I mentioned earlier. The conference was a turning point in the study. I have already described how my meeting with Patricia reshaped my research inquiry; however, the conference also proved helpful in other ways. The participant observation that I conducted at the conference was invaluable; some of the most compelling information I gathered did not come from the formal presentations but instead from the many informal conversations between practitioners.

My immersion in the field of crisis negotiation prepared me to appreciate the nature of the crisis negotiation discourse process. Going to the conference gave me credibility as a crisis negotiation researcher (particularly with Noesner at my side), and this contributed to my access to the Jefferson negotiation team later on in the study. Further, I was able to hone the research design and thus more sharply focus my inquiry. Although I was not formally collecting data at this time, after the conference I became saturated with information. Morse (1994) talked about saturation as "repetition in the information obtained and confirmation of previously collected data" (p. 230).

FIELDWORK AT THE JEFFERSON SITE

My fieldwork interviews with the Jefferson negotiators contributed to my research understanding about the setting of the event, the intricacies of what happened at the scene, and how each of the negotiators viewed the discourse process. In particular, the IPR interviews gave participants a way to revisit, in a vivid and direct way, their experience of the incident. Though the team

Table 2.1. Roles of Study Participants in the Jefferson Crisis Negotiation

Study Participants	Participant's Role in the Negotiation
Paul	Served as primary negotiator throughout the incident. Police officer in nearby city; trained as a negotiator.
Jane	Works in same police department with Paul, as 911 operator. Trained negotiator. Took copious notes and transcribed ongoing conversation in shorthand throughout the incident.
Ellen	Negotiator trainee; went with Paul and Jane to the scene as observer. Walked around scene as dialogue was unfolding and saw hostage taker's mother in school office.
Patricia	Sheriff's deputy in county where incident occurred. Not yet trained as a negotiator; served as observer and team member. Responsible for processing crime scene after hostage taker surrendered.
Don	Patricia's partner in the sheriff's office. Team member.
Bob	Trained and experienced FBI negotiator. Arrived at the scene two hours after incident began. With Jane, also served as a "coach" to Paul, sitting directly across from him at the negotiation team table. Paul described Bob as his "mentor."
Richard	Trained FBI negotiator. Only other person to talk briefly to hostage taker, early in the negotiation. When Richard identified himself as FBI, hostage taker hung up on him and later asked for Paul to return to the phone.

worked together to end the incident peacefully, each of them acted in a different capacity, with unique roles and responsibilities. They had different levels of negotiation experience and disparate perspectives on the process. See table 2.1 for a description of the roles of each negotiator during the Jefferson incident.

DESCRIPTION OF THE JEFFERSON PARTICIPANTS

The Jefferson negotiation team consisted of seven people from three different law enforcement agencies in three separate, but neighboring, communities. Paul, Jane, and Ellen came from a police department in a city neighboring the town where the incident took place; Patricia and Don came from the sheriff's office in the county where Jefferson is located; and Bob and Richard came from a nearby FBI field office in a large city outside the Jefferson community.

St. Olivia Police Negotiators: Paul, Jane, and Ellen

Paul was the primary negotiator. At the time of the incident, he was an officer in the police department and a trained negotiator. Jane was Paul's negotiation "coach"; that is, she served as his negotiation partner and backup. A 911 dispatcher in the same police department, she was the only one on the negotiation team who was not a police officer; however, she was a trained crisis negotiator. Ellen, a negotiator trainee, accompanied Paul and Jane to the incident as an observer. Paul, Jane, and Ellen arrived at the scene after hearing a call over the police radio. They went to Jefferson High School with the idea that they would assist other negotiators; however, shortly after their arrival, they were asked by the commander to conduct the negotiations with the hostage taker themselves.

I spent the most interview time with Paul, the primary negotiator. Over four separate interviews totaling ten hours, Paul discussed his experience of the Jefferson critical incident—at his home, at a local eatery, at Jefferson High School, and at a separate school where the parents of hostages waited out the siege. Jane was interviewed once, over the course of four hours, at her office on her day off. Still a 911 dispatcher, she was extremely helpful in explaining the details of the discourse; she had an amazing memory that served her well in the interview, particularly when I played the tape of the discourse. As Paul's coach, Jane had been intently focused on the talk. The interview Jane gave for this project was her first opportunity to talk about the incident.

Ellen, the team member who was a crisis negotiation trainee at the time of the incident, was interviewed once, for two hours. Now retired, Ellen possessed keen insight into how the incident affected her community. As an observer on the team with no other responsibilities, she had been able to walk around the school office. She had several interesting anecdotes about what she had seen. For instance, she was the only person to talk to me about the hostage taker's mother appearing at the school during the incident.

Lincoln County Sheriff's Office Detectives: Patricia and Don

Patricia and Don, detectives in the county where the incident took place, worked at the sheriff's office, only a few miles away from the school. They were among the first officers at the scene. Just days before the incident, Patricia and Don had been designated to become negotiators in their department; however, they had yet to receive training. Their roles on the negotiation team were as intelligence officers and observers. They provided important information that the others on the team did not have—information that proved essential to the negotiation.

Since the incident took place in their jurisdiction, Patricia and Don had more details about the investigative aspects of the incident. They knew more about its initial moments and its aftermath. In fact, Patricia, who was the investigator responsible for processing the crime scene after the incident was over, knew many facts about the criminal case. Several of these details had been relevant during the negotiation process, such as the size and layout of the room the hostage taker had used, the ammunition and weapons he had, and the exact path he took from his arrival at the school until the moment he surrendered.

Patricia gave an informative and compelling presentation at the crisis negotiation conference in South Carolina where we first met. Using slides, news videotape, and photos of the hostage taker and his victims, she gave me a better understanding of what happened at the incident. Unfortunately, she was out of town during most of my visit. We did meet on my last day, but she was volunteering at an air show and we had time for only a brief chat at a pancake breakfast in an airplane hangar. Instead of trying to talk over the airplanes flying above us, we agreed to conduct a full interview by telephone one week later.

During that call, I played excerpts of the negotiation dialogue for Patricia using the speaker function on my telephone. I recorded the exchange with the taping mechanism on my answering machine. Although the process worked well, this telephone IPR interview was not nearly as vivid as those I had conducted in person. In fact, it was cumbersome. I stopped it after two excerpts and focused on having a conversation with her. We ended up talking for several hours.

I interviewed Don, Patricia's former partner, several times during the week, for many hours each time. He provided useful, detailed information about the incident's management and aftermath.

FBI Field Office Negotiators: Bob and Richard

Bob and Richard were FBI agents and trained, experienced crisis negotiators. They had been trained separately, however, and years apart. Their FBI field office was an hour outside of the Jefferson community, so they arrived after the negotiation process had already started, approximately two hours into the incident and one hour into the negotiation. Each played a pivotal role on the team: Richard was the only other team member who negotiated with the hostage taker, and Bob had initiated a phone consultation with crisis negotiators at the FBI Academy that led to the development of a psychological profile, or personality assessment, of the hostage taker. The profile included specific recommendations on how to proceed with negotiations.

I interviewed Richard once, for two hours. Richard was the only other person on the team besides Paul (and Don, in the very first minutes of the incident) who actually talked with the hostage taker during the incident. Richard took over negotiations when Paul asked the hostage taker if he wanted to speak with an FBI agent. The conversation they had was a significant turning point in the negotiation. Now retired from the FBI, Richard has since earned his Ph.D. and is a university instructor.

Bob turned out to be one of the most generative of all the Jefferson participants. Several team members pointed out that Bob had played an essential role on the team. Paul even said that Bob had been like a mentor for him during the process. Bob had a tremendous amount of information and insight about the crisis negotiation discourse at Jefferson. He talked easily and confidently about the intricacies of crisis negotiation and was well versed in its philosophy and techniques. Retired from the FBI, he had many interesting stories about his work and his negotiation experiences.

I interviewed Bob twice. In the IPR interview, which was conducted in a quiet corner of a coffee shop over two hours' time, Bob, like Jane, gave detailed, vivid information about the discourse process. Impulsively, he drew a map for me of the negotiation room as the interview progressed. The map provided yet more information about the incident; I encouraged other participants to draw maps for me in later interviews, as well.

Participant Observation in the Jefferson Community

I met with the seven negotiators in a variety of locations—homes, offices, restaurants, and cafés. I went with them to places in the community that were relevant to the Jefferson incident. Don and I visited the memorial, which was near his home. Paul took me to the middle school where anxious parents had awaited the release of their children, and he also arranged to show me Jefferson High School.

At the high school, Paul walked me through the incident, starting from where the hostage taker parked his car and entered the school, continuing to the places he shot each of his victims and the classroom where he held the hostages, and ending in the hallway where he surrendered. Paul showed me the room where the negotiation team had worked, where police officials had set up their command post, and where the snipers from the SWAT team had positioned themselves. After the Jefferson High tour, I had a much more detailed picture of the actual incident. In the interviews that followed, I could clearly understand participants' descriptions of the scene and visualize their points of reference. Upon my return home, I rewatched a videotaped copy of a television movie that had been made about the Jefferson incident, which several participants had referred to, and saw it with a much more informed perspective.

When I was not interviewing or preparing to interview, I spent time at the local libraries in the community. I copied articles about the incident from microfiche files and sought out as much information as I could about it. I went to the local newspaper office, once accompanied by Paul, and bought reprints of important stories. During the times I was not with participants, I organized my field notes and listened to portions of interviews.

The period of time I spent at the site was extremely productive for the research. It improved my ability to comprehend the phenomenon I was focusing on. Furthermore, I found it fascinating to talk to the negotiators about their experience. They had so many interesting stories, ideas, and reflections on what happened at Jefferson, and they were extremely generous in sharing them with me.

The fieldwork helped me acquire a store of intuitive knowledge about this incident that was a great benefit in writing the study. To see the Jefferson community, walk around Jefferson High, and meet the negotiators provided me with knowledge about the Jefferson incident that I did not have before. I drew from this store of knowledge many times to tell the story of the talk and describe the process of how it unfolded.

Incorporating a Crisis Negotiation Expert

Gary Noesner participated in this study as an expert on successful, effective crisis negotiation discourse. My association with him gave me access and credibility in the field. In addition, he provided a wealth of information to me about crisis negotiation and sent me actual negotiation audiotapes to review. I involved Gary in the actual research process by interviewing him about his views of the Jefferson discourse. He was not involved in the Jefferson incident, but he was very familiar with the incident, the makeup of the Jefferson team, and the negotiation process at the incident. In fact, he had used the audiotape as a training tool at the FBI's crisis negotiation school. He also knew the two Jefferson negotiators who had attended the academy and made presentations on the incident.

As an insider in the field of crisis negotiation and an expert on the crisis negotiation discourse process, I decided to interview Gary to hear his views on the Jefferson negotiation process just as I had with the other participants. I conducted an IPR interview with him during a brief visit to the FBI Academy in Quantico, Virginia. This interview was productive in a different way than I experienced with the team negotiators. Noesner pointed out many things in the dialogue that I had not observed or discussed with the team members. He noticed specific communication techniques Paul often used, commented easily on how the discourse was constructed, and wondered aloud how he could use the IPR process to train new negotiators.

TRUSTWORTHINESS OF THE RESEARCH

A qualitative researcher strives to achieve trustworthiness by assuring that the study is accountable (Lincoln & Guba, 1985). In naturalistic inquiry, the researcher assures trustworthiness by addressing the study's confirmability, dependability, credibility, and transferability. Respectively, these four concepts relate to the quantitative research constructs of objectivity, consistency (reliability), "truth value" (validity), and applicability (Lincoln & Guba, 1985).

Confirmability

Confirmability rejects the concept of researcher objectivity and instead emphasizes the accuracy of the data themselves. According to Lincoln and Guba (1985), the primary way a researcher establishes confirmability is through an audit trail. An audit trail is a way to organize and document the research-in-progress, and it is also "a residue of records stemming from the inquiry" (Lincoln & Guba, 1985, p. 319).

There are five categories of organization and documentation in an audit trail. They are *raw data*, such as field notes and interview tapes; *data reduction and analysis products*, such as write-ups of field notes and preliminary concepts and hunches; *data reconstruction and synthesis products*, such as summary reports and the initial structuring of data themes, categories, and relationships; *process notes*, which refers to the researcher's thoughts about the method, design, trustworthiness or notes about the audit trail itself; and *materials relating to intentions and dispositions*, such as the research proposal and personal notes about the researcher's motivations and expectations, including a reflexive journal maintained throughout the inquiry (Lincoln & Guba, 1985).

My audit trail includes raw data—field notes, interview tapes, and written material that participants gave me (such as maps of the scene)—and process data such as text and audio journals and notes I took throughout my immersion process and my fieldwork at the Jefferson site. In addition, I included transcripts of my interviews with participants, a transcript of the IPR compilation tape, and a transcript of the entire Jefferson negotiation. The audit trail also includes things I collected—and often consulted—throughout the research process, such as instructional material on crisis negotiation (including an FBI manual and several training videotapes), and a copy of the television movie on the Jefferson incident. I continued to build the audit trail during the analysis process, adding notes on my emerging thoughts, ideas, and questions. I included a journal I kept during the transcription process, which was the beginning of my formulating both clinical and research connections, associations, and themes about the patterns in the discourse.

Dependability

Dependability has to do with the consistency of the study, rather than its accuracy. To demonstrate dependability, the researcher illustrates the process of "taking into account both factors of instability *and* factors of phenomenal or design induced change" (Lincoln & Guba, 1985, p. 299). Dependability is achieved through an auditing process. The audit trail helped me increase the dependability of the study. It illustrates the appropriateness of my inquiry decisions and allowed me to "identify, explicate, and support" the method shifts I made (Lincoln & Guba, 1985). According to Lincoln & Guba (1985), one comprehensive audit trail can determine dependability and confirmability simultaneously.

In particular, Noesner's assistance increased my efforts to keep the inquiry consistent. I often talked to him about the uncertainty I felt during the research process, particularly during the periods of my immersion in the field and my preparation to visit the research site. He was an important sounding board. He commented on what I noticed, and he offered his thoughts and ideas on things that puzzled, surprised, or intrigued me. I have several notebooks of our conversations.

Credibility

The credibility of a study refers to how the researcher shows that the data are representative of the multiple constructions about the phenomenon and that those reconstructions (made by the researcher) are "credible to the constructors of the original multiple realities" (Lincoln & Guba, 1985, p. 296).

I increased the credibility of this study through prolonged engagement with the phenomena, which was accomplished by immersing myself in the crisis negotiation literature and participating in multiple conversations with crisis negotiation practitioners, consultants, and researchers. I tried to learn about the field from as many different angles as possible. The familiarity I developed with the field and with the ideas circulating among negotiators helped me build trust and establish credibility with participants. For example, in one interview at the Jefferson community, a participant asked my opinion about the use of mental health consultants: Is it a good idea? What were people saying about it?

I further increased my credibility when I went to the setting of Jefferson and when I adapted my interview method to fit with participants' experiences.

By immersing myself in the crisis negotiation field, the Jefferson negotiation setting, and interviews with crisis negotiators, I was able to learn about the discourse process in complementary ways. These different practices helped me identify and assess both "salient factors and atypical happenings" (Lincoln & Guba, 1985, p. 307) in the phenomenon.

Other practices I used to increase credibility include peer debriefing, to explore "aspects of the inquiry that might otherwise remain only implicit" (Lincoln & Guba, 1985, p. 308); negative case analysis, which is a way of correcting and revising previous, erroneous hypotheses (Kidder, 1981, as cited in Lincoln & Guba, 1985, p. 309); and member checking, "whereby data, analytic categories, interpretations, and conclusions are tested with members of those stakeholding groups from which the data were originally collected" (Lincoln & Guba, 1985, p. 310). Lincoln and Guba called member checking the most crucial technique for establishing credibility (p. 310). I conducted member checks by going back to participants during the research process. I sent them copies of their interviews, for comments and verification, and I spoke with them on the phone, discussing my efforts at data reconstruction and themes emerging out of the analysis.

Transferability

Transferability has to do with the way the researcher accounts for how he or she reconstructs the data. In order to assure transferability, the researcher attends to the inquiry in a circuitous way, fully addressing both the phenomenon under study and the research process designed to study it (Lincoln & Guba, 1985). The researcher attends to both of these contexts so that the study's results are transferable for others interested in replicating the inquiry.

I attended to the study's transferability through the use of "thick description" of the phenomenon (Geertz, 1973). I worked at developing a thick description of crisis negotiation by my purposeful sampling of the negotiation audiotapes, incorporating an expert, conducting fieldwork at the site, interviewing the Jefferson team and utilizing the negotiation discourse in my interview method, and attending to self-of-researcher issues.

NOW WHAT? APPROACH TO THE DATA ANALYSIS

According to Chenail (1994), the qualitative research analysis process is, for the researcher, "a matter of pointing to a chunk of data and telling the reader what it is you are seeing" (p. 2). Defining it as a descriptive process, Chenail (1994) explained that analysis entails more than interpretation of the data—it also involves discussing the manner and means of the interpretation. Essentially, the researcher is saying: "Look at what I'm seeing. Here it is. This is what I think it is. What do you think of my thinking?" (p. 2).

Because crisis negotiation conversation is so contextually driven, I was interested in a parallel methodological approach. To analyze the talk, I purposely chose participants who could best facilitate my understanding of the discourse (Bogdan & Biklen, 1982). I examined the talk using my own lens as a clinician/researcher and also by including the voices of people present at the scene. Further, I included the perspective of an expert crisis negotiator who has widely influenced the field in my research. In these ways, I took a holistic approach to the study of the Jefferson discourse (Taylor & Bogdan, 1984).

Now I will discuss my research methodology, which I formally began after a yearlong immersion into the world of crisis negotiation.

THE FIRST STEPS: TRANSCRIBING

The first thing I did to formally begin the analysis of the discourse was transcribe the audiotapes of the entire Jefferson negotiation. This was an intensive and lengthy process, but was invaluable to my appreciation of the talk and its many complexities. As I transcribed, I could hear much of the interaction between the hostages and the hostage taker. I often found myself wondering about the interaction among the students, who laughed often, flirted with each other, and talked about the latest movies. When there was a break in the negotiation talk between Paul and Leo, I typed my thoughts about what I had heard alongside the actual discourse I was transcribing, calling this my "transcription journal." Later, several participants told me that they had wondered similar things about the hostages' demeanor during the incident.

After I made a complete transcript of the Jefferson negotiation, but before I went to interview the Jefferson team, I made a separate transcript of the five excerpts I had already chosen with negotiators for microanalysis. I took both transcripts with me when I conducted the fieldwork at Jefferson. However, this research focuses only on the content of the five excerpts on the compilation tape, which was the source of all IPR interviews. To fully explicate the discourse on the compilation tape, I referred to the conventions of conversation and discourse analysis. I noted the length of pauses, changes in intonation, and word emphasis. I marked changes in Leo's breathing pattern and the softness with which Paul uttered certain phrases. See table 2.2 for the notation legend I used to signify different features of the conversation. It is modified from Schenkein (1978).

Table 2.2. Notation Legend

(.)	Brief pause
(0.6)	Pause indicated in seconds and tenths of a second
—	Cutoff of prior word
=	No interval talk between the end of a prior and start of next part of talk
::::	Prior sound is prolonged; multiple colons indicate more prolonged sound
NO	Italics indicates emphasis; capitals indicate increased volume
!	Animated tone
hh	Breathing out
.hhh	Breathing in
?	Rising intonation
* *	Talk between is quieter than surrounding talk
> <	Talk between is faster than surrounding talk
( )	Transcription doubt
(( ))	Verbal descriptions
[[	Simultaneous utterances

THE SECOND STEP: COMBINING INTERVIEW DATA WITH THE NEGOTIATION DISCOURSE

I transcribed all of the participants' interviews over a period of two months. After I finished transcribing each interview, I printed it out and read it through one time. I made comments in the margins, noted ideas that came to mind, and highlighted what seemed important to my research question. I then put the interview aside and did not look at it again until all were complete.

Adding Participants' Data to the Discourse Text

All transcribing completed, I began a cutting and pasting process, adding each participant's views on the discourse to the five excerpts. This task required me to make distinctions about participants' data. The distinctions revolved around the relevance of the data to the research questions. When I was unsure about whether or not to paste a participant's comment, I went back to my research question(s) about what made the discourse successful. I asked myself: Does this comment tell me something about what served to facilitate or undermine the relationship? With this as a criterion, I could make consistent and informed choices about those parts of the context of the text that belonged in the analysis.

It is important to note that decisions about what to cut and what to paste required little decision making regarding the participants' IPR interviews. As participants had made their IPR comments about a specific bit of negotiation discourse, I simply pasted each participant's IPR comment exactly at the moment of the discourse where the participant spoke. In the ethnographic interviews, however, it was not so easy. Participants had talked more generally about the negotiation, bringing up important points that contextualized the negotiation but were not necessarily related to the discourse. I had to decide whether or not to paste this data and, if I chose to do so, where to place it in the text. I placed ethnographic comments as close as possible to the negotiation talk to which they referred.

A note for the reader regarding the upcoming analysis: where a participant's comment is from the IPR interview, I have noted the stop number and the page number. The former indicates the number of times the participant had stopped the tape. For example, "Jane, 07, p. 14" would indicate that the comment came from Jane's interview, it was the seventh time she stopped the IPR tape, and her comment is on page 14 of her interview. When there is no number after a participant's excerpt and only a page number, the reader can safely assume that the excerpt originates in an ethnographic portion of the participant's interview.

Distinguishing Relevant Data

Cutting and pasting finished, I found I had a document that consisted of the five negotiation excerpts plus the participants' comments about those excerpts. Essentially, it resembled a transcript of a group interview about the negotiation, with all of the participant's voices present. Before I began to include my own research voice in the text, I edited the voices of the participants. My goal was to develop a coherent narrative of the negotiation, particularly the story of how the process of the talk unfolded.

THE THIRD STEP: CREATING A STORY

My third step was to create a cohesive narrative of the document. This is where my formal analysis began, as it is when I began to make interpretations about the discourse process, based on participants' comments about the discourse, when compared with what was observed in the discourse analysis. I made distinctions, connections, and interpretations about the text and the context of the text. An example: Several participants referred to their intense concentration, or "focus," at specific points in the talk. This told me I should closely examine that excerpt of the negotiation. In a different example, several people discussed Paul's calm voice affecting the hostage taker, with regard to a particular sentence they each had noticed. Looking at the text, I could see how the hostage taker's voice was softer; it was reflected in his speech.

During this step, my voice as a researcher/clinician became more explicit. As I wove my voice into, around, and in between the participants' voices, I created a story about the talk. What follows in the next chapters are microanalyses of five pivotal moments of the Jefferson High School crisis negotiation.

NOTE

1. All Jefferson negotiators are renamed in this study.

Chapter Three

The 1st Moment: 4:25 P.M.

Don is one of the first officers at the scene, along with some of the SWAT team from his department. He is also the first negotiator to arrive. However, Don's designation as a negotiator in his department has only been in effect for a few days. He has not had the opportunity to attend formal training. Nevertheless, he will become responsible for beginning a dialogical effort.

Although Don does not know exactly what has happened at the school, he is aware there has been a shooting and that the hostage taker remains inside one of the school buildings. Don is in the precarious position of a first responder at the scene. He has to simultaneously prepare for either assaulting the hostage taker or beginning a dialogue with him. Not knowing which way the incident will go, Don and the SWAT officers approach the Arts Building, where the shooting has just occurred. They wade through a group of students running outside of the building, some covered with blood, and walk inside the school.

> The first room we just happened to go into immediately to the left was Mr. Grant's classroom and he and Julie Denny were down in that classroom. So here they are, you know gun smoke is still in the air. There's people screaming and crying and we don't know where the shooter is; we know we got a shooter, we know he has a shotgun, there's shotgun shells. (Don, p. 7)

Don and the SWAT officers walk to the middle of the building, stopping at the foot of the staircase there. Unbeknownst to them, the hostage taker is overlooking the staircase with a riot gun. Although Don and the others cannot see the hostage taker, they can hear him:

> He's up there, he's yelling, he's still very jacked up. He's yelling, he's emotional, barking orders screaming at these kids the kids are crying. (Don, p. 9)

Don and the SWAT team prepare for an assault up the stairs. However, the assault does not take place because the hostage taker starts to communicate with Don.

> He put one of the kids on the stairs and we started talking, ... we started to communicate. Once we developed dialogue, our plan at that point is if he starts to shoot again, we have to go. ... Once we started dialogue, I'm talking to the kid on the stairs he's talking to the other kid, and we're just kind of talking back and forth and that went on for a while and then ... I started talking to him and trying to calm him down and he's coming down a little bit and I said, this is not working, let me get a phone to you and we can communicate. This yelling back and forth is not going to work and our voices are going to go bad. Let me get a phone to you. So I negotiated the delivery of the phone, and he agreed to accept the phone. (Don, p. 11)

Don heads over to the administration office to set up the command post and negotiation room. He is met there by his negotiation partner, Patricia, and the negotiation team from St. Olivia (Paul, Jane, and Ellen), who arrive after responding to a request for mutual aid on the police radio. Commanders at the scene ask Paul and Jane to conduct negotiations, since they are trained and have experience in other incidents. Paul and Jane agree to be primary negotiators. Then, all five set up negotiations in the vice principal's office. Shortly after, the two FBI negotiators, Bob and Richard, arrive at the scene and join them.

The first conversations Paul has on the throw phone are with a hostage named Alan. While Paul is talking to Alan, Paul can hear the hostage taker in the background, threatening the students.

> Up to this point you're hearing him directing people. He is basically orchestrating that room, using his shotgun like a conductor would use the wand and moving them. He's moving the people in the room. And when he talks to the girl about going to the bathroom and coming back, he points the gun at her, and then he points the gun at her, the girl next door, and says you don't come back I'm going to shoot your very best friend. (Paul, 02, p. 44)

The first excerpt of the analysis is actually the second conversation between Paul and Alan. The first conversation, which took place about 4:20 P.M., was very brief. In that conversation, Paul asked Alan questions about where the hostage taker was standing and how many people were in the room. Alan's response was to repeat verbatim Paul's question to the hostage taker, who was apparently right next to him. Now, in the second conversation with Alan, just a few minutes after the first, Paul asks similar questions about the hostage taker. In response, Alan is completely silent. The team finds Alan's participation in this way very frustrating.

The 1st Moment: 4:25 P.M.

Attending to how they talk to Alan is one of the team's first tasks as a group. Mistakenly, they assume that Alan will know how to talk to the hostage taker on their behalf. After their first conversation with Alan, the team realizes Alan has his own experience to deal with.

> I had to come to grips with the fact that even though I'm there to help this kid and he should see that, I thought automatically he would recognize, the police are here to help me. Well, it came real quick to me that, no, he doesn't see the police as a help to him. He sees the police as complicating the problem. If the police weren't here, this guy would leave, he might go home. He in fact probably is more endeared to the person holding the gun than he ever would be to me. . . . It makes him a liability to us, because we don't know if we can trust him. (Paul, 02–03, p. 45)

> It's *frustrating* cause it's like, God, you know . . . this is somebody you're going to have to be real careful with, in case he *does* say something you don't *want* him to say. More so than somebody you *think* is doing okay, you know, so it's *kind of* frustrating. . . . You really have to choose your words carefully. (Jane, 11, p. 37)

The team reconfigures their approach toward talking to Alan. In the first excerpt I present, the team instructs Alan in how to talk to the hostage taker. Also, Paul tries to find out some information about the situation in the room. During the call, the hostage taker can be heard in the background, yelling at the hostages and asking Alan what the police officers are telling him.

BEEP ((The negotiator calls and a hostage picks up the phone))

PAUL: Alan?

ALAN: What.

PAUL: Is the guy st—standing there?

ALAN: Yeah.

PAUL: Okay. He's close to you?

HOSTAGE TAKER (HT) [to Alan]: What's he saying!

ALAN [to the negotiator]: He wants to know what you're saying.

HT [to Alan]: (.) Tell him right in front of about forty people.

PAUL: Alan, Alan.

ALAN: What.

PAUL: *Never* tell him what I'm asking you. Do you understand?

ALAN: I do.

PAUL: Okay.

ALAN: ((silence))

PAUL: If he asks you if I'm asking you something, make very sure he does not know what it is. Even if you have to lie to him. Do you understand?

ALAN: ((silence))

PAUL: Okay? This is very important. We're trying to help you. But you have to help us. Do you understand that? Okay . . . is there *any way that he will talk to us*? Ask him if he will *talk to us* now.

ALAN: They want to know if you'll talk to them.

HT: What?

ALAN: They want to know if you'll talk to them.

The hostage taker comes to the telephone for the first time. After Paul introduces himself as a negotiator, the hostage taker asks Paul what police agency he works for. The fact that he asks this kind of question gives the team some initial insights about him. They begin to suspect that the hostage taker sees himself as having special knowledge.

> He's from here. He wants to, I think he's trying to, are you local? Are you FBI? Who am I talking to? What's your role in this? What's your title what's your status. Kind of to set the pecking order, to see if he's talking to a professional. . . . Who am I talking to? Am I talking to the *sheriff*? Am I talking to a *captain*? Am I talking to an *FBI special agent*? You know, you have to understand, I picture him, swelling up. (Don, 03, p. 14)

> I think it kind of gave him, well he wanted to know and I think it gave him an indication of who was all out there. Will they bring someone from St. Olivia? Oh, okay. I think that that really does bring a lot of focus into just his knowledge of what's out there, in his tactical mind if you will. (Paul, 12, p. 69)

HT: Tell him . . . go ahead, follow each other. You go down there. If you don't, I'm gonna shoot your friends. (1.0) All right, go ahead bring the phone over here.

ALAN: All right, hold on.

HT: Yeah.

PAUL: Hello?

HT: Hello.

PAUL: Hi, my name is Paul Baker.

HT: All right who are you?

PAUL: I'm a negotiator for the police department.

HT: For what, St. Olivia or Steubenville?

PAUL: For St. Olivia. (0.2)

Paul offers to help the hostage taker, and the word "help" leads the hostage taker to unexpectedly tell Paul about the relationship he had with Mr. Grant, the teacher he has just shot. He gives the information freely, with minimal inquiry from Paul. He mentions words like "pass," "flunked," and "grade," and associates them with the fact that his "dreams" were knocked down. These words are markers for the team, particularly for Paul.

> It was almost like when he said this, the lights went on, the bells rang, it was like here is the handle. It was handed to me, just as big as could be. And I thought, let's run. Let's run big time. When he said that Mr. Grant messed up his life and that Mr. Grant gave him a failing grade, and that ruined all his dreams, it was a hook, a big hook, it was I mean it was something that sometimes you don't get for several hours into the negotiations. (Paul, 05, pp. 45–46)

PAUL: I'm here to try to help you.

HT: (hh) Yeah.

PAUL: Okay?

HT: Know Mr. Grant tried to fuckin' help me too.

PAUL: Who's Mr. Gant?

HT: Mr. Grant.

PAUL: I'm sorry, Grant.

HT: Yeah, he tried to help me he tried to help me fuckin' pa:ss. And he fuckin' flunked my ass with *one* fucking grade. Fucking knocked everything down all my fucking dreams.

PAUL: [[Okay it seems like (0.1) it's *very* apparent to me that this upse:ts you. And I'd like to I'd like to=

HT: =Upset me? It ruined my fuckin' life!

Paul responds to the hostage taker's revelations with a reflective comment: It's apparent to me this upsets you. Two participants (Bob and Don) told me it is a "textbook" negotiation response. However, the comment is inappropriate.

Its timing (minutes into the negotiation discourse) is premature. Further, its banality sounds condescending; the referent with which it is associated (a mass shooting) is anything but banal. Thus, the comment is unproductive. It is no surprise to hear Leo immediately yell at Paul: "Upset me? It ruined my fuckin' life!"

Further, Paul makes the reflective comment without pausing before he makes another statement: "It's very apparent to me that this upsets you. And I'd like to—I'd like to—." The second part of the sentence signifies a solution attempt. Paul is trying to solve the problem with very limited information. This is unacceptable to the hostage taker; he interrupts Paul to tell him how seriously his life has been affected by flunking school.

Paul's response indicates to the hostage taker that he does not understand the severity of the situation or the nature of his problem with Mr. Grant. Interestingly, Paul relates strongly to what the hostage taker says, because it is a situation familiar to him. He, too, had serious difficulties as a student.

> When I saw that, and knowing my situation, it was, this is the bond. This is *the* bond. That's gonna work. I mean there was no doubt in my mind, it was like a gift from God. If you can, you know. Manna from heaven if you wanna use the biblical term. (Paul, p. 48)

Because of this shared experience, Paul is confident that he can easily talk to the hostage taker. His confidence leads him to feel that he has a special understanding of the hostage taker's history.

> The hook was just, it was *huge*. It was and the only reason it was huge was because we had a similar situation. Anyone else who had never suffered what he had suffered would have never been able to pick up on that clue but it hit me like a huge hammer. (Paul, 06, p. 49)

The rest of the team also notices the value of the new information. For Jane, the hostage taker identifies a problem that the team can address after they establish a relationship with him.

> That was a good indicator of at least some of what may have been bothering him. You could tell by the language that the failing grade made a *big* effect on his life. (Jane, 02, p. 34)

Similarly, Bob realizes that the revelation about the teacher is meaningful.

> [Paul] started off with you know, *exactly* what he should have started off, to *let* him talk, to find out *why* he did it, and that's what's going on here. I mean all of a sudden now we know why, Leo's relationship with the teacher that he killed. (Bob, 02, p. 42)

In the next sentence of the exchange, the hostage taker gives more information to negotiators about what precipitated his behavior. He is reflecting further on his earlier statement, about how flunking Mr. Grant's class knocked down his dreams. Here, he indicates what those dreams involved—a job, a diploma, money, college, and a prom date. He relates the loss of those dreams to the fact that Mr. Grant flunked him. It appears obvious that he wants to talk about what happened. Yet, rather than encouraging this discourse about the past, Paul tries to focus attention on what is happening right now.

> HT: You try to get a fucking *job* around here without a diploma. How else am I gonna get enough money to fuckin' survive on let alone (.hhh) try to go to fucking co??llege. I had everything planned, I had the fucking prom, I had a date, I had everything. And he fuckin' blew it away.
>
> PAUL: Okay. (hh)
>
> (0.2)
>
> PAUL: It's obvious that I can't change *that*, but I am here to help you *today*. Is there something that I could do to help you TODAY?

Paul says it is "obvious" he cannot change what happened in the past. Use of the word *obvious* adds a hint of condescension to the statement, potentially slighting the hostage taker's experience. Trying to focus on the current situation, Paul uses the word "help" again, connecting it to the word "today," which he repeats twice. These are good words to use, and Paul will repeat them later. However, their use here is a problem. According to Gary, Paul's problem-solving statement is untimely; it comes before there is any indicator of rapport.

> To some extent I could see the beginnings of some efforts to problem solve. And it's probably a bit early for that. "Why can't we start over now?" or "I can do something to help you." Those aren't negative in that they will cause a problem, but they're probably not the most maximum responses that you could engage in to begin the rapport-building process which will be required to occur before you can get into the problem solving. (Gary, 07, p. 4)

According to Gary, Paul could ask open-ended questions at this point, allowing the hostage taker to elaborate on what he has said.

> Obviously something just triggered this young man's activities, and he wants to talk about it. He's certainly angry at his teacher and he's talking about at this point what we seem to know is he feels his teacher has spoiled his life. And you want to get some more information about that. (Gary, 07, p. 4)

In the next sentence, the hostage taker asks for what he wants—a chance to tell his story—in another way. He requests a news reporter. This request leads the team to conclude that the hostage taker has a "message" that he wants to share with a public audience. The team will carry this idea, "He has a message," as a theme throughout the discourse. Further, the team assumes that by asking for the media, the hostage taker sees himself as an important person, worthy of recognition.

> Talking about wanting the reporter, that was kind of when we were looking at, he wants that kind of, that self-importance. What's he looking at here? Why does he want a reporter? What's the message he wants to tell the world? And again that's something, he's trying to get a message out. What's the message and *why*, so that was that was kind of a clue for us, to see what else he had to say. (Jane, 03, p. 34)

Along with his request for the news crew, the hostage taker says other things that confirm what the team has begun to suspect: that he sees himself as an expert on law enforcement and tactics.

> He thinks in his mind that he knows law enforcement because he's read law enforcement books. You know, tactical books. Magazines and this is the mindset. . . . It's like me going to read a book on how to play golf and me thinking I'm a golfer. Exactly. When I know nothing about golf. But in his mind he thinks he knows what we're all about and what makes us tick. (Don, p. 15)

HT: Yeah, you can send up those fuckin' (.hhh) you can send up those uh, r-reporter, and I said I want 'em with shorts and shoes on nothing else except a camera and I want two of 'em (0.1) and they better not be fuckin' cops.

PAUL: Okay, well, we're not, (.hhh) we're not gonna play any tricks on you okay? That is the number-one ground rule.

HT: 'Cause I know your fuckin'— I—I—I know know your tactics, I fuckin' studied you all my fuckin'— (.hhh) I—I've been into war stuff since I was a little kid. I know every fuckin' trick you guys play, all right, so don't *fuck* with me.

Paul assures the hostage taker there won't be any "tricks," and the hostage taker repeats the word "trick." The hostage taker's statement is an attempt to set the "rules" for how he wants things done. It illustrates opposition to Paul. However, by using Paul's word *trick* (e.g., "I know every fuckin' *trick* you guys play"), the hostage taker also demonstrates, subtly, agreement with Paul's characterization.

At this point, there is now a discernible pattern in the hostage taker's manner of speech. His agitation is illustrated in his heavy inhalations and exhalations and in his repeated use of the word *fuck*. In the next excerpt, Paul attempts to de-escalate the hostage taker's intensity by avoiding repetition of the word *fuck*, changing it to *screw*. Paul and Gary referred to this as "softening" the language.

> One of the techniques hostage schools taught you is always soften the words of the hostage taker. Okay.... The first key was soften his words. (Paul, 06, p. 47)

> Typically we would we try to move away from those kinds of words because they tend to perpetuate anger. We try not to sink to their level, or to repeat words that might just further inflame . . . we try to soften it up a little bit. (Gary, 04, p. 3)

As Paul softens the language, he also tries to reassure the hostage taker that the people at the scene only want to help him. He has now used the word *help* more than five times, and this time, he refers to the "helpers"—to "we," not "I." The use of "we" broadens the helping effort from Paul to other people. It will also prove useful later for another reason, which I will discuss in a moment. After a silence, the hostage taker quickly changes the subject.

> PAUL: Okay, hey nobody's here to screw with you, okay? All we wanna do is help you (.hhh) and we need you to kind of help us a little bit.
>
> (3.0)
>
> HT: Yeah, well wh—why did you take so *fuck*in' long to get the fuckin' (hh) *keys*, I wanna know. Why'd it take so fuckin' long??

Before Paul answers the question about the keys, he makes a statement and then asks a question of his own—can he address the hostage taker by name? Paul's intent is to develop rapport with the hostage taker; he is not concerned about knowing the hostage taker's true identity.

> In this case, it doesn't matter the name. The identity is so important because it brings you a step closer to gaining a good communication with this guy. . . . If you can get this guy to give you a name, I don't care if it's the right name . . . it's something to call him. . . . The big issue is to be able to *talk* to this person, and call him something besides air. (Paul, 07, p. 50)

Paul's question promotes an interaction between the hostage taker and the hostages, as the hostage taker asks the kids to come up with a name. Immediately someone yells out "Leo!" and the kids laugh in the background. The fact that the hostage taker asks the students for a name, and that they answer him and laugh about it, gives the team information about what is happening inside the room. It proves to be an unexpected bonus for them.

> It got him communicating with the kids. What, well they wanna name, well what about the name? You know can you give me a name? And they come up with

"Leo." And then they laugh. After he tells me who it is. They're laughing because, we're pulling the wool over somebody's eyes. (Paul, p. 50)

See there, the laughter in the background, could be an indicator, that, even though he's got control of the people, he's got the gun in there, gave it a little, what do I want to say . . . a little less of a serious mode, at that time. I mean they were laughing, he didn't seem to care that they were laughing. You know, somebody think of a name, "Leo," oh, ha ha ha . . . you know, he didn't care that they were laughing it was almost like, I mean I know they weren't, it was almost like they were in it together. (Jane, 05, p. 35)

PAUL: Okay. I—I—I'd like to answer that question for you and I *will*, but can I have some sort of a name to call you (0.2) so I'm not just talking to—

HT: No, you don't need a name.

PAUL: Well, I don't care if it's your *rea:::l* name or not.

HT: Psst ((tells the students to come up with one, someone yells out "Leo!")).

HT: My name is Leo.

PAUL: Okay Leo.

HT: All right?

PAUL: Okay.

((Laughter among the students))

The team finds the information about the atmosphere in the classroom useful. The hostages appear safe and in relatively good spirits, so the team is more relaxed. They feel they can pay full attention to the negotiation. For some team members, though, the interaction among the kids is disconcerting, because it is such a contrast to the shootings that have just taken place:

You hear these kids. Some of these kids, they're clueless. They don't have any idea what's happened downstairs. And sure there's a guy up there with a gun but he, but they're . . . they didn't know what had gone on. A couple of kids did because they'd been downstairs but not everybody knew. And they had no concept of their own mortality. Because they don't know. Even afterwards they're laughing and joking, some of them, but some of them it was devastating to them. Very emotional, I heard of one that went home went in their house and months later hadn't left their home, still there. You know, incredibly emotional. But I, you can hear them laughing in the background. God if you only knew what happened downstairs you'd be a whole lot more afraid of this guy. (Don, 06, p. 16)

Paul begins to use Leo's name immediately, and he will do so generously throughout the night. That he accepts it without question, and appears unconcerned about its accuracy, further builds his relationship with Leo. In the next excerpt, Paul starts talking to Leo as if they have just been introduced. He will repeat both their names, and then he directly answers Leo's earlier question about the location of the bathroom keys, explaining why they "took so long" to locate, using Leo earlier phrase. Also helpful here is that Paul continues to use the word *help* and introduces two other words that he will repeat often, in a variety of different ways, throughout the negotiation: *understand* and *peaceful*.

Paul says that the reason the bathroom keys took so long to find is because of chaos at the scene. According to Gary, Paul's directness about the police activity is much more effective than giving a vague answer.

> Negotiators will typically say, "We're working on it, we're working on it," and that really doesn't provide much of a response to the subject's stated desires. And what Paul has done here is come up with a very logical reason for the delays and that's chaos and confusion. And it's just right along with what we teach. Blame the obvious. It's difficult for us to do what you want right now because I mean there's confusion and chaos and people rushing here to remove kids or whatever it might be. That's very good to do that. And the subject understands it. He can see it for himself. (Gary, 05, p. 3)

Paul adds that the chaos is due to an effort to resolve things peacefully for Leo. In other words, it is a way to "help" him. In a very subtle and effective manner, Paul obtains Leo's agreement with this statement. This begins a conversational pattern Paul repeats often: Paul makes a statement, adds a slight question, waits for Leo to agree, then confirms the agreement.

> PAUL: Leo, my name is Paul and (hh) the reason it took so long to get the *key* is you have to understa*::nd* if you put yourself in the place of everybody out here there's a lot of cha::os goin' on, okay? So we're—we're working here as a *team* to help *you*. So that we can resolve this thing peacefully. Do you understand that Leo?
>
> LEO: I understand.
>
> PAUL: Okay.

Paul introduces a new topic at this point in the talk. He tells Leo that he may not have to go to prison for what he has done.

> PAUL: Now, if I can help you do that, and now, the thing that I was trying to explain (0.2) through the young man on the phone before is that things aren't as serious as they seem. There are ways that I can he:lp you. You know I heard you over the phone saying that you were afraid that you would have to go to state prison. That may not be true.

LEO: S . . .

PAUL: Now LIsten to me Leo. (0.1) It's true. It may not be true. Okay?

Leo begins to reply but Paul interrupts him, saying, "Listen to me Leo. It's true. It may not be true. Okay?" Paul's statement is a way to tell Leo that it is correct that he may not have to go to prison. While the sentences express this idea congruently, the manner in which Paul makes them is confusing. At first glance, the statements appear to contradict each other.

At this point in the talk, Paul has already achieved some important goals. He has elicited a precipitating event, a name, and an agreement. In the next sentence, he will try again to connect to Leo's experience. He will try to convey understanding by paraphrasing Leo's situation as "bad raps" in life. Paul uses the word "obvious" to preface his statement. The comment will not fit for Leo. In response, he repeats earlier markers, about flunking the class and lacking the grades to pass. This time, however, in addition to saying Mr. Grant "blew it out of the water," Leo comments even more strongly on how his life was changed—it was "destroyed."

PAUL: It's obvious that you've had some bad raps in life.

LEO: Bad raps? They totally fucked up my— ((says to hostage "I want those . . .")) Bad fuckin' raps? With *one* fuckin' class you fucking destroyed someone's life I tri??ed my fu??cking hardest every fucking day tried to bust my ass to just get enough grades to pass and he fuckin' blew it out of the water.

By characterizing Leo's experience as "bad raps," Paul underestimates Leo's situation. In the next excerpt, Leo tries to rectify Paul's misunderstanding. For Jane, Leo's attempt to help Paul understand shows that Leo is interested in having Paul hear his story.

See, he's interacting with him, he says, "I understand you've had some bad raps . . ." "Bad raps! You know, lemme tell ya about it!" He's interacting with him, he's open to talking to him. It's like, "Yeah I wanna, oh, well I wanna tell ya about this, let me tell you about my side, you know, I wanna tell you what happened." (Jane, 06, p. 35)

In the next exchange, Paul repeats that Leo's problems are in the past and tries to bring the talk to "today," this time using the word "now." However, for Leo, the problem is *not* in the past—it *is* happening right now. He has tried to tell Paul how his previous situation affects his current life. Here, he will try again. This time, Paul makes a slight variation to his comment. He steps back from his earlier position of trying to solve the problem right now. Instead, he asks Leo about the *possibility* of trying to solve the problem immediately. The less restrictive question will open up the dialogue.

Before he can respond, Leo sees something that causes him to leave the phone. Leo and Paul share a polite nicety at this moment, indicating a social aspect of their interaction and showing that the relationship is progressing.

> PAUL: Okay Leo, (.) that's in the past now. What's in the future is what we can do *now*.
>
> LEO: They expect me to go to fuckin' Steubenville and drive there every fuckin' three three nights a week— I didn't have a fucki??n ca??r.
>
> PAUL: Okay.
>
> LEO: All right? I just fuckin' got a car.
>
> PAUL: All right. (0.3) So why can't we start now Leo? (0.3) I mean what's— what's the reason we can't start now?
>
> LEO: Hold on a second.
>
> PAUL: Su::re.

At this point in the negotiation the team members start to notice a difference in Leo's responses to Paul. Paul's calm approach is affecting Leo.

> You hear [Paul] calm him down? He's listening to Paul. There comes a point where his breathing slowed way down. Now you know the anxiety and the judgment pendulum is starting to balance. Because his breathing, and he's breathing real heavy in the phone, it's like okay okay and he's hanging on every word you know he's going uh-huh and he starts to acknowledge, yeah, uh-huh, he's listening, it's like, oh yeah this is good, this is very good. (Don, 07, p. 17)
>
> [Paul's] also calming him down. His tone of voice, he's not trying to bullshit him, he's not trying to, he's just, very calm, which calms him down. He doesn't make any mention about his language, he doesn't criticize him for anything he says. (Bob, 05, p. 44)

Paul's responses are unlike what Leo may have expected to hear from police. Leo cannot argue with someone who is not offensive to him.

> One of the real effective things of the negotiator here is his tone and his demeanor are very appropriate. He projects sincerity. And willingness to help. And presents a profile that is probably very unlike what the subject expects from a policeman. [Interviewer: "Which would be more . . . ?"] Authoritative, confrontational, demanding, rigid, sterner voice, you know, "Okay you better do what we say," "I

want you to put your gun down right now." Instead he's getting pretty empathic responses from the negotiator here and it's effective. (Gary, 06, p. 3)

Jane, as the secondary negotiator on the team, is attending very closely to Leo's tone as well as his words.

> You want to listen to [Leo's] tone cause there were times where he is upset, he is agitated, there are times he came down, in his tone, and so you want to listen to the person's tone as well as to the words they're saying. (Jane, p. 18)

Furthermore, Jane is transcribing the talk, as it is ongoing, using shorthand. This will help the team process the talk during breaks in the conversation. It also will result in Jane noticing numerous subtle nuances of the conversation between Paul and Leo. For example, she attends to changes in words and tone, as well as when the changes occur.

> [Leo] sounds like he's calmer now, so then you try to go back and try to remember what it was that may have calmed him down, it could have been a number of factors but you try to remember what calmed him down in case he gets agitated later you can use that same wording, that same verbiage to bring him down. (Jane, p. 19)

Paul is using a benevolent tone of voice, and the fact that this contrasts with what Leo expects contributes to its effectiveness, as Gary suggested. The unexpected nature of the response, and the context in which it is given, is disarming, and that is a benefit to all negotiators. In this case, it marks the team as different from other people in Leo's world. Leo has stated that he couldn't even get his teachers to listen to him; now, he has a team of police officers listening to his problems.

In the next excerpt, Leo will see something else that disturbs him. Paul uses Leo's discomfort as an opportunity to establish himself as a liaison between Leo and the outside "chaos and confusion." Paul is managing the larger system that Leo has to deal with in the incident. Increasing the range of his role, from negotiator to manager of the chaos and confusion, Paul also adds to his maneuverability. He becomes useful to Leo in multiple ways.

PAUL: Hey Leo? Leo?

LEO: What?

PAUL: Listen, if you see something *out* there that up*sets* you, you tell me and I'll make sure that they're not there to upset you. [[Do you understand that?

LEO: [[I'm serious. I don't want no fuckin' snipers, I don't want no SWAT tactical units, I don't want no helicopters (.hhh) going above, fucking landing 'em on the top and you pulling down. (0.1) I don't want nunna that shit. (0.3) I *know* your guys' tactics, I *know* how you fuckin' work. All right?

PAUL: Okay. I understand that. And we—and we wanna work with you. So (0.1) if you see something that makes you uncomfortable, I'm the guy that you talk to and I'm the guy that helps you, okay?

If Leo responds to Paul's invitation to come to him with any problems, there will be an implicit agreement that a helping relationship exists. It is this sort of implicit understanding that can pave the way toward ending the incident cooperatively.

To have somebody like Paul say we want to work with you, he's just saying, I'm the guy that's going to get you out, that's what he's saying. I'm the guy that's going to help you. Nobody else can help you but me. Then, Leo knows that this is his *out*. If he can, he has Paul, then he can get out. (Bob, 06, p. 44)

According to Gary, Paul's efforts to manage the confusion also serve to keep the potential volatility of the incident in check.

Right now if the subject responds violently to something he sees or something he suspects or something he's scared about, it could change the whole dynamics of the incident. Of course in this case, there were already dead people. But what you want to do is to undertake those measures or efforts that keep him away from further violence. So what the negotiator's done here is very good. He said if you see something out there that bothers you, or you're concerned about, and he's saying that because he just prior heard the subject say, "Is there something goin' on out there? Is there somebody moving?" So the negotiator is quite properly intervening at this point in time and saying basically saying, we are not here to do any of those things, but if there's something *you* see, let me know. (Gary, 08, p. 4)

In a more subtle way, Paul is characterizing his talk with Leo as "in here," something distinct from what is happening "out there." Also, Leo says all the things he does not want, and Paul says he "understands" and wants to "work" with Leo. *Work* is synonymous with *help*, a word Paul has already used generously. These statements help Paul portray himself as a person who wants Leo to be comfortable, at ease, and free from upset. In this way, Paul sets apart the context of the talk from the context of everything else at the scene.

In the next sentence, Leo utilizes Paul's helpfulness by asking about what is happening outside the building. Paul will subtly not answer Leo's question; however, Paul's response is posed forthrightly and it acknowledges Leo's inquiry.

48   *Chapter Three*

> LEO: All right, how many—how many cops you got out there, how many police cars?
>
> PAUL: Well, there's a there's a lot of us.
>
> LEO: How many?
>
> PAUL: I—I haven't counted 'em, Leo, I really haven't.
>
> LEO: I don't want—I don't want the SWAT tactical team *arou::nd* here at all. I'm serious, if I see anybody in black or anybody with a *fuckin'* gun (.hhh) I'm gonna shoot two people. And I::: really don't wannu, but fuck it, you *know* I— you only get fed up with so many thi:::ngs so much, you can only have so many disappointments until you break. All right?
>
> PAUL: Okay.

When Leo asks how many cops are outside, Paul says, "There's a lot of us." He aligns himself with the police at the scene, and this is a potentially dangerous thing. It has the effect of placing Leo in an opposing position, which the team does not want. Soon, Paul adjusts this position and realigns himself with Leo, marking himself as different from other police at the scene.

Leo's response to Paul in the previous exchange is interesting in that it begins as a threat, but ends on a personal note: Leo feels broken by disappointments. Paul focuses on the latter in his next comments. He will note Leo's desire for no more disappointments and make a subtle suggestion that the incident can end in a nondisappointing way.

This next exchange is compelling in other ways. Using Leo's frame of "no disappointments," Paul ties together language and themes from the earlier discussion. Additionally, Paul broadens Leo's problems to include "everybody else." This is a reference to the ongoing incident, which is a "problem" for everyone at the school, including Leo. When Paul states the hard work he and Leo can do to resolve the problems, he includes Leo as a participant in the solution. Paul uses the word "we" to signify those participants. By the end of the statement, "we" also includes Leo. The entire exchange is essentially an offer to Leo, and he takes it.

> PAUL: Leo, I don't want you to have any more disappointments either. And believe me, it's *not* too late. If you will work with me and you will work—work *hard* with me here, we can resolve *your* problems, okay? And we can resolve everybody else??s problems. Isn't *that* what you'd like to do?
>
> LEO: Yeah.
>
> PAUL: Okay. Now.

Paul uses the same conversational pattern mentioned earlier to obtain Leo's agreement to end the incident. Further, each time Paul introduces a change or a new idea, he paces it with Leo by making sure Leo agrees with it. In this case, Leo's agreement to solve "everybody else's problems" is an important indicator for Bob.

> We were making progress already. This was within the first hour that I got there. And as I said, even at the time we were up there, it was like to me it was like a textbook, like I was reading it out of a textbook, the things that he was saying, the things that he was doing. (Bob, 07–08, p. 45)

Similarly, Gary sees the agreement as noteworthy because it results in Leo's committing to the negotiation process.

> That was a very powerful ... question ... on the negotiator's part. "We can solve your problems, we can solve everybody else's. Isn't that what you'd really like to do?" I mean, I think that was very clever or intuitive of the negotiator to ask that question because he vested the subject in reaching an agreement there. (Gary, 10, pp. 4–5)

For Paul, the agreement illustrates a shift in Leo's view of the incident. And if Leo's view of the incident can change, so can his view of how it may end.

> Once I get him to agree, mentally he's made a change. If he says yeah, I don't want that to happen either, he has now gone from the killer mode to maybe, I don't wanna kill. Maybe, I don't wanna do this. . . . I've taken him down a level, he's willing to work with us. (Paul, 11, p. 60)

If Leo sees the incident in a narrow way, his range of choices will be limited. Similarly, if his view of the incident becomes broader, so will his range of choices. Now, with this agreement stated, there are increased options for how to end the incident. One of these options—a voluntary surrender—is exactly what the negotiators will hone in on later.

At this point, a theme of talk is developing, and so is a pattern of teamwork. During breaks in the conversations, they process what has been said. But while Paul is on the telephone, the team intently focuses on what they hear. During the conversation, they are writing notes to each other, communicating with their faces, with their eyes, and on paper.

> We didn't—we didn't talk [while Paul was on the phone]. Every once in a while we wrote notes. Gave it to him. I think I wrote quite a few that were just real short, you know, like, "*Good.* Keep this." Nothing, not telling [Paul] what to do, sometimes it's my recollection that he would write, shall I—shall I continue, on that line? And then we would write *yes*. (Bob, 09, p. 45)

You're brainstorming, brainstorming, brainstorming, brainstorming. Where are we going to go, what are we going to say, don't touch this, let's try this, no that didn't work let's try that, you know, what does he respond to? Praise. Oh, he responded incredibly well to praise. (Don, 19, p. 25)

We'd toss ideas around each other, as one of us would hear something, even by facial *expression* or maybe a little note to the other one: Did you hear that? Or could you make out what that was? (Jane, p. 16)

[There was] a lot of sign language, a lot of facial, I remember. Sticky notes, a lot of sticky notes. I mean, I have—we have yellow pads and big pencils and big pens and we make notes and put things up, you know, "Don't go there!" or we'll mark it in red pen, or you know, and you're makin' notes and flippin' pages and you—it's like you can hear the paper rustling, cause they're going good, good, good, ask him this, this, and this. It worked. It works very well. Because everybody's inputting information, us, the FBI, for the most part, most of us were in the room, and we're brainstorming information and we're whispering and talking and changing notes and going, Don't go there, bad, good, good, great, great. (Don, 08, p. 18)

We're talking amongst ourselves, pretty much in normal voices: Well, did you notice he was talking about this? . . . It gives you stuff to work with him on when you go in later. And then, just like with everything else, every person's going to interpret things differently. Or somebody's going to hear something somebody else didn't hear. So yeah, did you catch when he said—? Oh no, I didn't, but that makes sense! I'll bet that's why . . . you know. So yeah, the brainstorming's real important. (Jane, 09, p. 36)

It was quiet. Nobody was yelling. There was no yelling. People were conversing in normal ones, but you could cut the tension with a knife. It was just so so strong, just so strong. . . . Everybody was worried. We all came together in that room. . . . There was a lot of talking and then the notes. We'd write notes and just make quiet recommendations as to what to do. (Patricia, p. 7)

At this point in the talk, Leo has become calmer, has discussed the precipitating event that brought him to school, and has agreed that he wants to end the incident peacefully. Now, Paul furthers the progress of the talk by self-disclosing that he also had problems in school. It is a subtle self-disclosure; however, the response from Leo is tremendous. Leo's lengthy and detailed reply shows Patricia that he is ready to talk to someone.

He admitted he had problems in school, and he didn't learn as fast as the other kids, and he just—and he talked about, you know, like, without a diploma you're nothing, you can't get a job. . . . I think all this depression he'd gone through, from the time he'd been laid off . . . I think this just kept building and building in him. I think he was totally devastated when he walked into the school that day. (Patricia, 03, p. 16)

PAUL: Why don't you tell ME now it's obvious that, uh, that you've talked about (0.1) not making it through school which is— (0.1) you know, there's a lot of us, there's a lot of us that's had a tough time in school. Believe me, *I* did.

LEO: Yeah.

PAUL: *I di::d.* I had a real tough time in school. So I understand that. But it's not too late.

LEO: See, I have a learning process. I could learn stuff but it takes a little bit longer than some people and a lot of teachers just—just didn't understand. They didn't take the time to sit there and teach me. And *that's* one of the biggest fuckin' problems. It was like people like Mr. Grant. He could pass all, he just looked at me, fucking goes >*You didn't pass*< and just like walked on, like no fuckin' nothing, like no fuckin' no big deal, and he just totally ruined the fuckin' kid's, uh, uh, whole life just like he was nothing. He didn't sit down and talk to me about it or nothing, he just said >*You didn't pass*<. That means you don't graduate, you don't, if all the shit you had with the prom, it's all the fuck out the door, everything. And how do you think my *fuckin'* parents felt about it— they're fuckin' just lookin' at me saying, well maybe we can send you to college. Yeah right, how am I fuckin' supposed to get there? Walk?

For Gary, this exchange indicates an important change in the balance of discourse content. It also signals a difference in the interaction between Paul and Leo.

All the conversations up to this point in time, the subject had been basically providing warnings and venting his anger. Now all of a sudden, he's just started to talk to the negotiator about something totally unrelated to the ongoing conflict. Which speaks to the very origin of why he's doing what he's doing. . . . He already feels comfortable enough in this *very* short period of time in this *extraordinary,* volatile situation because of the demeanor of the negotiator and his presentation as being someone genuine and interested. This guy's already feeling comfortable enough to share with him something kind of personal. "I could learn a little bit more than some people but a lot of teachers didn't understand me and . . . ." I think that's a really significant shift. (Gary, 12, p. 5)

For Paul, the revelation from Leo further solidifies a personal connection. In fact, the words Leo uses vividly remind Paul of his own experience as a student.

He had a learning disability. He couldn't retain information. He blames that on the fact that teachers wouldn't take time to sit down and *explain* to him, about what needs to be done. He basically says, they don't care, and *then* he says basically that they have an attitude of he's very worthless. Here's your grade, you didn't pass, you know, you're *stuuupid*! . . . They might as well walked up there and hit him with the paper and said, You are the stupidest person I've ever met in my entire life. That's *exactly* the type of thing he felt. And I'm here to tell you, I know *exactly* how he felt because those words were said to me. (Paul, 12, p. 61)

The above quotes illustrate the negotiators' attempts to make sense of Leo's behavior according to the contextual information he gives about it. They are trying to understand the situation from Leo's perspective. Up to this point in the negotiation, Paul has relied on his personal experience to guide his negotiation efforts. However, the connection Paul feels is not yet productive in the talk. According to Gary, though, a personal connection to Leo is unnecessary; rather, what is required is a concerted effort to be curious about what he says.

Rather than just saying "I understand," it would have been better to just demonstrate understanding by feeding back some of the things he said. . . . I think the negotiator— I don't think this is a criticism, but probably would have been more effective to feedback to that right away rather than try to say, "There's some ways we can help you with that." *That* will come. But maybe, maybe a bit later. . . . I mean that preceding paragraph, from the subject, had a lot of strong clues in it. The teacher just— part of it's respect, a lack of respect . . . he felt the teacher gave him, and he was mistreated. The teacher had just come up to him and said, "You didn't pass," that's all he said, "You didn't pass." He repeated it twice. . . . What his words are telling you is, the way that occurred certainly stuck in this guy's memory and for all time. . . . I mean, these are things that created some tremendous emotional scars for him. (Gary, 13, p. 6)

In this next excerpt, a continuation of the previous talk, Paul does something different. Prior to this point, Paul has always made himself or Leo the subject of the sentence (e.g., "I can't," "We can't," "You've had"). The first couple of statements in the exchange are also in this vein, and they are ineffective. Leo merely mumbles a response. At this point in the talk, however, Paul changes his way of conveying understanding to Leo. He takes the statement outside of the negotiation; that is, he talks about the teacher. In the last sentence, he makes a reflective comment that communicates his understanding from another perspective.

PAUL: *I understand. You know, there are some ways that we can help you with, uh, college. There are some ways that we can help you, uh, with finishing high school.* ((Leo mumbles something)) It's obvious that the teacher did not understand you.

Paul uses the word "obvious" in a way that benefits him; the condescension it signifies is now directed at Mr. Grant. By saying it is obvious that the teacher did not understand Leo, Paul conveys interest in a different way than he has thus far. He is sending a message of "I understand" to Leo by literally saying that the teacher *didn't* understand him. Paul is now *showing* understanding rather than *claiming* it.

> LEO: ((Laughs)) He understood me. He understood me for a yea??r and a ha??lf. I had him—I had him in two other classes.
>
> PAUL: You know, *I* had some teachers like that also. They just absolutely didn't understand (0.1) what my limitations were, (0.1) and didn't work with me. You know, it sounds like you have the same problem with *this* teacher.

Leo's laugh after the previous statement is sarcastic, and his reply laced with irony. Leo's irony and sarcasm indicate that he knows Paul understands that Mr. Grant, indeed, did not understand Leo at all.

Paul uses self-disclosure again, hinting that he also has a story about school problems. In the next excerpt, however, Leo will tell Paul that there is more to his situation than school problems. Paul does not want to pursue other topics with Leo, so he tries to prevent this conversation. Instead, he offers to help. However, since Paul does not allow Leo to say more about his problem, the offer of help is premature. How can Paul help if he does not know what the problem is? Leo's response is to try to end the conversation.

> LEO: *Yeah, it wasn't just that. It was all the other fuckin' disappointments in the world.*
>
> PAUL: [[Sure.
>
> LEO: [[People::, all that crap.
>
> (1.0)
>
> PAUL: Leo, (1.0) I wanna do everything I can to help you here. So why don't we work on a solution. Would you like to do that?
>
> (3.5)
>
> LEO: Well, . . . just give me some time to think.

Leo response seems to indicate that he is overwhelmed. In fact, he is likely highly physically and emotionally aroused. The team appears to recognize that Leo is overwhelmed; however, some also attribute his reluctance to talk at this juncture to other factors.

> He's heard some of what Paul's saying and it's too much for him to absorb, so he has to sit and really think about what he was told. I think it made him feel

54   *Chapter Three*

good that someone was willing to listen to him, and to try to work out some of the problems. . . . He does need time to go think about, absorb all this. (Jane, 08, p. 36)

What's happening is I'm overwhelming him. I'm giving him so much information about, I understand, you know they didn't understand you. I'm talking about the teacher didn't understand you, I had teachers like that that didn't understand me, that didn't know my limitations. [Interviewer: "And it overwhelmed him, you think, to hear that from you?"] Sure. You know, well, he can't process at this point, you have to understand he's got a limited learning ability. He can't *process* information that quickly and assimilate it into reason that quick without having to think about it. Mull it over and that sort of thing. And I really think that he had a real difficult time just absorbing what I was saying. He understood it. He just wasn't absorbing it. (Paul, 13, p. 70)

I think it was just that his thought process was slow. He's not real quick. Not very bright. He's just not very bright. He has limited gray matter and it's just obvious from listening to him. I mean, you're not dealing with a Ted Bundy here. (Don, 17, p. 24)

Leo again attempts to end the conversation by telling Paul when to call back. He prefaces his statement with an announcement that he is going to hang up the phone.

> LEO: >and I'm gonna hang up now< (.hhh) and I want you to call back in ((as if looking at watch)) (2.0) five fifteen, okay.
>
> PAUL: Can—can we make it just a little bit sooner Leo?
>
> LEO: Uh, (0.1) five ten.
>
> PAUL: Five ten.
>
> LEO: Right.
>
> PAUL: Okay, uh, that's about twenty minutes. How 'bout if we call you back at, uh, say three minutes after five. . . . That gives you about ten minutes.

Leo is arranging the next contact and that is a positive sign. The negotiators do not want to wait too long until the next call. When Leo suggests a time, Paul immediately works to make it sooner. Paul offers to talk not at 5:15, as Leo suggested, but at "three minutes after five." Paul's offer is precise and this illustrates directness and a commitment to speak again.

Instead of answering Paul's comment about the time or trying to hang up again, however, Leo asks Paul a question. He wants to know where Paul is located.

LEO: Where are you located at?

PAUL: I'm sorry?

LEO: Where are you located at? Which part of the, uh, surroundings are you located at? Are you in the main office? Are you outside? Are you in a van?

PAUL: Well, I'm (.hhh) ((as if to laugh))— I'll be honest with you. I'm from St. Olivia and I've *nev*er been to Jefferson except for today so I'm not sure *what* the building's called.

LEO: Well, are you in the front office?

PAUL: Ah . . . it looks like an office, but I couldn't tell you if it's the front one or not.

By answering that he is in an office, but he is not sure which one, Paul effectively manages Leo's challenge to him; he answers the question but does not give his location. Paul avoids the question for an interesting reason: he wants to dissociate himself from the school.

> I didn't want him to think that I was so far and lofted. I didn't want the office because it's always been such a negative thing to students. I didn't want him to think that I was in the office in the ivory tower judging him. I wanted him to think that I was new, I was thrown into something, and here I am to help. (Paul, 13, p. 72)

Leo seems to accept Paul's statement; the issue of location goes no further. Instead, Leo tries to end the conversation. He repeats the time of the next call. The time he gives is the earlier time that Paul had suggested. For Gary, that is important; it illustrates the "seeds of willingness to cooperate."

> The negotiator's persistence there got the guy to back off from sort of a deadline. . . . A lot of times a subject will view that as a powerful thing. I said fifteen after, and that's what I meant. Yet in this case the negotiator was able to back him down. It may seem like a small thing, but it already shows the seeds of willingness to cooperate and to be a little flexible. . . . You don't want to press too hard, it's not a major issue that you want to get in a big argument over. But he backed him off, he won himself the ability to call about ten minutes earlier than the subject initially wanted. It's a small thing but it's symbolic. (Gary, 16, p. 7)

LEO: All right, okay, call back [[at—

PAUL: [[how 'bout—

LEO: A::t five minutes after::: uh five.

PAUL: Five minutes after five. Okay.

LEO: All right?

Leo moves the time two minutes and Paul accepts that. This shows progress in the relationship between them; the compromise allows them both to save face and demonstrate flexibility.

Still, the discussion continues further before Paul and Leo hang up. In the next sentence, Paul reiterates his position as a consultant for Leo. He then obtains Leo's agreement, once again, to allow him to participate in this role.

> PAUL: Leo? Listen, if you have any problems at all, you pick up that phone and you call me and *I* will do something.
>
> LEO: [[(((Leo says something))
>
> PAUL: [[Would you do that?
>
> LEO: What the-e number?
>
> PAUL: All you have to do is just pick up the phone, =it'll ring. Now listen, Leo.
>
> LEO: =All right
>
> LEO: What?
>
> PAUL: If you see anything, before you take *any* action at all, you call me and allow me to have the opportunity to fix it, okay?
>
> LEO: All right.
>
> PAUL: Would you make that deal with me?
>
> LEO: All right.
>
> PAUL: Okay Leo, thank you.

Paul invites Leo to initiate the next call. He puts it very clearly in Leo's hands: "if you have any problems," "you pick up that phone," "you call me," "if you see anything," "before you take action," "you call me," "you allow me the opportunity to fix it." By making so many statements with Leo as the subject, Paul suggests that Leo can take an active role in the negotiation. In combination, the efforts in this exchange convey respect as well as the expectation that further conversations are not only forthcoming but also inevitable.

The team notices that Leo has made a "deal." Bob sees that Paul now has a "promise" from Leo. Ellen sees that Paul has been able to "take him down." Gary concurs with these comments and observes that the agreement is enhanced by Paul's repetition of Leo's name.

> See, that was nice. The negotiator did a very appropriate thing, "Before you do anything, you call me first. Do we have a deal on that?" He basically said yes. And you notice that the negotiator's using his name a lot even though he knows it's not his true name. He's calling him Leo, he's calling him Leo, almost every time he

says it. And I suspect the negotiator will try to inject his name back in there as much as he can so the subject begins to hear it and starts using it and that's all very good. You know, "Would you make a deal with me. All right?" The deal is that I'm not gonna do anything until you do this. And it's good, it's the beginnings of give and take, it's coming to an agreement that both sides can try to accommodate the other's needs. That's an important psychological step. (Gary, 17, p. 7)

Despite Leo's repeated attempts to end the discussion, the current conversation continues. Leo reminds Paul about the request for news reporters and explains why this is so important to him. Notice that by the end of the exchange, Leo stops using strong language to make his point.

LEO: Okay, (.hhh) and, uh, I want you to make sure about those fucking, uh, news people. I want them *he::re*, okay?

PAUL: 'Kay, Leo. As you understand, there's a lot of problems out here and it's taking some time and I *pro*mise you I am checking on that. I'm having *my* people here check on that. (.hhh)

LEO: All right, I'm not gonna come in here and shoot 'em or anything. I just wanna talk to 'em (.) I wanna explain that what some of the pro??blems that some of the kids have here that the teacher's just showing off like its nothing.

PAUL: Um hmm.

LEO: All right?

Leo chooses to explain why he wants to talk to reporters, and this illustrates that he feels respected by Paul and trusts Paul. He assumes Paul will want to know this information. Recall that Paul has established himself as a consultant. Leo's offer of a reason why he wants to talk to reporters and his explanation of how he will treat them shows he is already participating with Paul in that role.

Paul has successfully positioned himself as someone working for Leo. Thus, Leo is in the position of having someone working on his behalf. Leo is in a different role now; he has a say in what can happen in the incident. This positioning is useful to the discourse and will be important at a later point in the negotiation.

The next excerpt is the end of the first phone call between Paul and Leo. After several attempts to hang up, Leo finally ends the conversation by repeating the time of the next call.

PAUL: You understand, Leo, that there aren't any television stations in St. Olivia–Steubenville. They have to come from out.

LEO: I know, Walston or Greenwich. I know.

PAUL: And, uh, and this time—this time of day with the traffic and everything, it takes a *lo:::*ng time. Be patient with me, I'm working as hard as I can for you. Okay?

LEO: Okay, uh, five after five.

PAUL: Okay Leo. [[Thank you.

LEO: [[All right.

PAUL: [[Thank you very much.

LEO: [[Okay.

PAUL: Bye.

((End of call))

Chapter Four

The 2nd Moment: 6:00 P.M.

The first phone call between Paul and Leo at 4:25 P.M. was only ten minutes long. Despite its brevity, however, it was productive. Two hours would pass before Paul and Leo speak again for this length of time. When Paul calls back at 5:05, Alan is on the line; Leo refuses to come to the telephone.

Several important things happen after the 4:25 phone call. The students locate a radio, because Leo wants to find out if there are any reports on the incident. They also locate a television. The students hook it up, but the reception is poor. Also, the air conditioners in the room stop working and the students begin to get uncomfortable. In addition, Leo asks the hostages if they want pizza. They agree, "Yeah!" and one student yells out, "Charge it to Mr. Grant!" The students laugh.

The request for pizzas gives the team a legitimate reason to try to get Leo to the telephone. They call repeatedly to ask for details and specifics: How many pizzas? What ingredients? What kind of soda? How much soda? Cups or bottles? Despite the negotiators' persistence, Leo does not come to the telephone; he has the hostage Alan field these questions. Leo says he will talk to the negotiators only after the pizzas are delivered.

The team is very concerned that Leo is refusing to talk to them. They make a decision. The next time Leo gets on the line, at about 5:20, Paul quickly asks him if he would like to speak to someone "from the government." Leo agrees, indifferently. Similarly nonchalant, Paul does not elaborate further. He quickly returns to asking for details about the pizza. He tells Leo he is not sure ten pizzas are enough. Can Leo tell him how many kids are inside? Leo says that there are 84 people with him. The team does not believe it.

Paul introduces the idea of speaking to someone from the government because he and the team feel another negotiator might be able to do a better job. In particular, the team pins their hopes on one of the FBI agents.

> Paul was doing all right with him at that point, but it didn't really seem like they had *meshed* that much. Which a lot of times, it does. It takes a while to get that bond built up, so we discussed having one of the FBI agents get on. (Jane, p. 12)

Jane's comment indicates she understands it takes time to develop a bond with the hostage taker. However, introducing a new speaker means that even more time will be needed for a *new* bond to develop. The team has not fully considered this. In addition, by changing speakers, they deal with their concerns about Paul's relationship with Leo externally, that is, outside of the conversational process. Changing speakers is a way of changing the process of the talking and, for that reason, could be productive. However, changing speakers also requires adjusting to a new relationship. For that reason, it is inefficient.

From Gary's perspective, the team's decision is unnecessary; in his view, they are doing an excellent job.

> If I'd been the negotiation coordinator, I would have under no circumstances switched a negotiator there. Because it's clear to me that, particularly mindful of the violence which had already occurred in this extraordinarily high-risk situation, that was probably about as good a negotiation as you could have. I mean, it's just stellar. (Gary, 18, p. 7)

Another factor influences the team's decision to change speakers. They are encouraged by the presence of Bob and Richard, two experienced FBI agents and seasoned crisis negotiators. Paul and Jane, the primary negotiators at the scene, are vividly aware of how helpful it is to have Bob and Richard on the team.

> Well, we both felt relieved when the FBI showed up because, you know, when you got to talking to Richard, I mean, God, his credentials are fabulous. . . . I mean, the man has been there, done that. You know, Bob Bixby the same way. And it's like, Yes! Let these people do their job. Do their magic. (Paul, p. 22)

> I couldn't even tell you at what point that Bob Bixby and Richard Rogers walked in. . . . I saw two guys walk in with briefcases and suits and I knew it was the FBI and it was like, oh good! ((Laughter)) . . . And it was interesting because they walked in, and just because they were dressed in suits, I guess something clicked. And I knew right away where they were from, and they're

here to help and we can use any help and I'm sure that they're more experienced in this and it was almost a relief when I saw them walk in.... We've got help here.... And somebody who's probably more prepared for this caliber type of thing. (Jane, p. 12)

The team's uncertainty about their progress is heightened by concern about the seriousness of the incident. They assume that the FBI agents have more experience with incidents of this size and thus can do a better job. According to Gary, this is a misconception among negotiators, as well as an error on the part of Jefferson negotiation team.

It's a confidence level and most police departments—they may handle a lot of suicides and domestic and barricade situations, but it's relatively infrequent that any department in the country handles something so volatile like that. I mean, there's been children killed. And it's a school. The whole community. It's a big, big, big thing, and it's as every bit as significant as anything the PLO ever did on an airplane. It's a big thing to that community. As well it should be. And despite all these very unique and critical elements here, he's done just an absolutely superlative job and now to bring in a new negotiator, even if he's a good one, would be very inadvisable.... In [Leo's] mind, comparing talking to the two of them, he's going to want to talk to who he's more comfortable with. It's human nature. (Gary, p. 8)

Another factor that contributes to the team's decision is their conclusion that Leo will want to speak to the FBI. Since Leo requested a news reporter, they believe he sees himself as an important person. They assume that by offering Leo an opportunity to speak with the FBI, they are addressing that perceived need.

See, the media was a big deal to him, we thought, so we thought, well, maybe if the media's a big deal, maybe he'll think an FBI agent is a real big deal. (Jane, 11, p. 36)

You know, we're thinking at this point, he wants the big white father from Washington, D.C., to come out and save his butt, you know, Efrem Zimbalist Jr. flies in, you know, we had that opinion at that point. This is what this guy wanted. And we got that from [him] asking for the news reporter. (Paul, 14, p. 73)

That was a strategy; we thought, Leo was talking to the spokesperson, the hostage negotiator, from St. Olivia; let's pump his ego up, let's give him the big guy, let's give him the hostage negotiator from the FBI. We wanted to pump up his self-esteem and his ego by letting him talk to the man from the FBI. We thought maybe that would work better than just a guy from St. Olivia. (Patricia, 04, p. 20)

The team is on the right track in terms of trying to understand how Leo perceives the negotiation. However, their assumption that the FBI will make him feel important is faulty; it is based on *their* view of the FBI agents, not Leo's. In fact, Leo feels threatened by the law enforcement presence at the scene; he is wary of them. Apart from asking for news reporters, Leo has never asked to speak to anyone else besides Paul.

Richard agrees to take over dealing with Leo, and his negotiation is technically smooth; in fact, he repeats almost verbatim what Paul has already said to Leo. However, as Gary pointed out, it does not matter what Richard says or how he says it. Leo already has a relationship with Paul. Richard, who will listen attentively and respond appropriately, is nevertheless a new person to talk to.

The talk starts out uneventfully; Leo is calm, as he was previously with Paul. Soon, however, Leo becomes angry and explosive. He begins to use old phrases, such as "I don't want" and "fuckin' SWAT."

PAUL: Leo, I'm gonna put Richard on the line. He's an FBI agent, 'kay?

LEO: All right. Put him on the line.

PAUL: Hang—hang tight, here he comes.

LEO: ((Silence))

RICHARD: Leo.

LEO: ((Silence))

RICHARD: My name's Richard. I'm with the FBI. I—I wanna try and help.

LEO: ((Silence))

RICHARD: Are you there?

LEO: Yeah.

RICHARD: How ya doin'?

LEO: Well I'??m doi??n' oka??y no??w but . . . (someone's gonna get it) if those fuckin' pizzas don't get here.

RICHARD: (.hhh)

LEO: I'm fuckin' serious (.hhh) and I don't want no fuckin' SWAT tactical units, no FBI guys flyin' around here, 'cause I *know* your fuckin' tactics. I studied 'em all my life. I'm fuckin' into guns and war. *DON't* fuck with me, okay?

RICHARD: I, uh, absolutely will not.

LEO: I want no fuckin' special units with helicopters landing on top. I don't want no fuckin' snipers in *any* of the windows. I've got over *eighty* people here. (0.2) All right? And I don't have nothing to fuckin' lose!

After just a few seconds of talking with Richard, Leo is heated and agitated. He begins to posture in a similar way that he had earlier with Paul.

> The negotiator's voice is very soft and appropriate. Sounds very soothing, and that's good. But what does the subject do? He jumps right back into his threats. I think he would be less likely to go through that again at this juncture with the former negotiator. They've already covered that ground. But now because you've got a new person on there he feels compelled to restate the parameters of his security again, which actually kind of serves to inflame him. You hear his voice get angry again. (Gary, 19, p. 8)

> He just exploded . . . just the three letters "FBI" seemed to be enough to set him off and start it all over. Now we have to start all over. Now he's venting. (Richard, 04, p. 8)

In the next exchange, Richard tries to calm Leo down by offering to manage the outside activity. His offer to manage the chaos is similar to what Paul has already said. However, Richard poses the offer slightly differently, his voice is more authoritative, and his choice of words is different (one noticeable absence is the word "we"). Richard comes across as an expert who has control over the incident, rather than a consultant working on Leo's behalf.

> RICHARD: Okay. Well, the—the people that are he::re are very, very *concer::ned*, but they will do nothing until (.) I give the word, so if you will work with *me::* to get this thing worked *out*, I can guaran*tee* you that there will not be any SWAT operation and nobody'll get hurt. (.) So just, uh, maybe you can tell me a little bit about what—what—what's goin' on. (.hhh) How can I help?

Shortly after this exchange, at the end of Richard's first phone call to Leo, the SWAT team rescues a group of students on the first floor. The rescue itself is not reflected in the transcript or the discourse; the team learns about it only after it occurs, by hearing Leo's reaction. Although Richard is unaware of the rescue, Leo later suspects otherwise. According to Paul, Richard's earlier comments, in the context of this rescue, serve to discredit him.

> Richard said, there are many, many people here, and they will do nothing until I give the word. Well, what happens while Richard's talking to him? The SWAT team goes and extracts those kids. What did he just tell the hostage taker? I'm the guy that controls things. He killed himself. As far as Leo was concerned, Richard gave the order for those SWAT teams to do what they did. (Paul, 15, pp. 74–75)

Leo restates his request for a news crew, but Richard does not address or answer this statement. Remember that Paul, while not actually answering the questions, had at least been addressing them in some manner. Richard, however, completely ignores Leo's request. Instead, he asks about the exact number of hostages in the room; Leo says he has close to eighty people inside. Hearing this number a second time, the team begins to believe it is possible Leo is telling the truth.

> LEO: >Well, one thing you can do, you can send, uh, the camera guy< Channel 3 *peo*ple and >I want 'em in sh*orts* and I want 'em in *sne*akers and I don't want nothin' on 'em and I don't and, uh, and I want 'em here in (0.4) less than an hour<. All right?
>
> RICHARD: Well, (.hhh) you have, uh— Tell me again how many people you have? Eighty?
>
> LEO [to hostage]: About eighty . . .
>
> RICHARD: About eighty people?
>
> LEO: Little over eighty.
>
> RICHARD: Okay. (.) (.hhh) Well, that's too many people for any one person to manage. Whyn't you send some of those people out?
>
> LEO: Oh, no, I don't think so. First of all, they give—give away my tactical position and I don't want that. (.hhh) (.) Also, I—I think I can handle 'em all. All right? And when those pizzas get here, they'll be pretty set up. Okay. So I want those pizzas (.hhh) and I want those cokes here cause these fuckin' people are getting hungry. And I fuckin', [[I
>
> RICHARD: [[okay
>
> LEO: I want you to call back in half an hour.=
>
> RICHARD: =Well . . .
>
> ((Leo hangs up))
>
> RICHARD: Are you still there?
>
> ((End of call))

Richard suggests that Leo has too many hostages to manage and tells him he should send some out. While this comment is made nonthreateningly, its content, given the previous discussions, is potentially problematic. Leo has already described feeling disrespected as a student; now Richard is implying he may not perform well as a hostage taker, either. Further, the comment is not structured as a question but is posed as a statement. Although the comment appears relatively benign, in the context of Leo's life, it may have been perceived by him as a lack of regard for his ability. He responds as if he has something to prove.

The above exchange was Richard's first phone call as negotiator in this incident. He later has two more conversations, one with Leo and one with Alan. The second conversation is similar to the first; Leo hangs up furiously after repeating his request for a reporter. In the third conversation, which Richard initiates just a few minutes after the second, Leo refuses to come to the phone. Alan fields that call.

Richard makes the third call to tell Leo that a medevac helicopter would be taking people to the hospital. The call is a preventive measure. Richard wants to let Leo know about the helicopter before he hears it and becomes upset. Alan takes the information from Richard.

It is during Richard's third call that the team hears Leo say to Alan, "I don't like this guy. I wanna talk to that other guy." This remark is the first indication to the team that Leo has formed a bond with Paul.

> At some point, Leo said that he wanted to talk to Paul again and then we knew that he had bonded with Paul and that was a *big* plus, because the bond had been made and that was a good thing. (Jane, p. 12)

When Leo says he wants to talk to "that other guy," the team realizes Leo has bonded with Paul. This information gives them a sense of progress.

> We knew we were heading in the direction we wanted to go at that point. We had a bond established between him and the negotiator; it was kind of comforting cause ... when he asked to speak to Paul again.... [We knew] this is a good thing, this is good. (Jane, p. 12)

> [Leo] said, "Can I talk to that guy from St. Olivia?" And he and Paul had really established a rapport and I think a lot of that had to do with Paul saying, yeah, I had the same problem, the teacher's didn't understand, I know what you're going through, and he had struck a chord in him and that's what we had to go back to. And Richard never got on the phone again, and neither did anybody else 'cause he had hit it off with Paul and so we didn't want to mess with that. Once he asked to talk to Paul again, we weren't going to mess with that; we left it with Paul. (Patricia, 04, p. 11)

Paul also recognizes the implications of Leo's statement:

> After the SWAT team had inserted and got those kids, the trust between Richard Rogers and Leo had *ended*, there was *none*. He did not want to talk to him. He asked for the guy from St. Olivia and wanted to talk to them.... I didn't know I had any rapport with him until he asked for me. (Paul, p. 19)

The team displays great flexibility in that they calibrate themselves so quickly. Once they know what works, they continue in that direction.

You just wave a flag and try a few things to see what works, keep track of what seems to be working. (Richard, 07–08, p. 10)

You don't keep trying to jam it down their throat. If it doesn't work, you try something else. You know you've got to think really fast on your feet, and I think that's one of the things that really helped in this case, is that we had so many people on the team, thinking of things, and suggesting things, and what one person didn't think of somebody else did. (Patricia, p. 21)

Well, when we tried the FBI agent, it didn't work. There was no rapport. It was going nowhere. We had to go back, back on track. . . . Paul was doing a good job. He was doing a good job, he had Leo's trust. (Ellen, p. 11)

Interestingly, it is Jane who is most aware of the potential of the discourse process at this point.

It was a good thing to know that that bond had been formed because then we could really get down to working out a solution to get *him* out of there, get the kids out of there safely. . . . But it just, all started seeming to kind of fall into place. Like I say, you never know for sure what direction a person's going to take, and it still was a lot of work to make sure you kept on track, but on an overall basis, it seemed like then from that point—I don't know, but to me that was, to me that was a big sigh of relief, it was a *big plus*. It just, it's like, Yes. This is good. ((Laughter)) [Interviewer: "Like downhill from there kind of?"] No. No. We still—we still had a lot of work ahead of us, but it was just a real positive accomplishment for us at that point. (Jane, p. 20)

Chapter Five

The 3rd Moment: 6:15 P.M.

In between Richard's third telephone call and Paul's return to the telephone, Leo surprises everyone by releasing a group of twenty students. Alan phones the team to tell them about this; the students are already walking out of the Arts Building when the call is made.

In the next exchange, Paul expresses gratitude for this gesture. He talks with Alan briefly before Leo comes to the telephone.

ALAN: He said that he'll let some more people go.

PAUL: Okay. That's—that's fine. We just wanted to thank him for letting those people out now.

ALAN: Okay, he wants the pizza here right now.

PAUL: Okay, the—the FBI guy said that he wanted to talk to me. This is Paul again. Does he want to talk to me now?

ALAN: Uh, yeah. 'Kay, hold on . . . he said he'll talk to you in a minute.

PAUL: Okay. We'll hang on here. Everybody comfortable?

ALAN: Yeah. Looks like it.

PAUL: How—how are you doin', Alan?

ALAN: Good . . . just standing here . . . ((inaudible)).

PAUL: No—nobody entered—injured in the building right now?

ALAN: No.

PAUL: Okay. Everybody—everybody seems to be okay?

ALAN: Yeah.

PAUL: Did you get the fans working?

ALAN: I'm a little bit scared.

PAUL: Sure, I can understand that. And, uh, you're doin' okay?

ALAN: Yeah.

PAUL: All right. *You're doing a very good job for me, Alan. I really appreciate that. Okay. I know it—I know it's tough in your position, okay? I know it's real tough and you're doing a great job* (.) Okay they just confirmed that the pizzas are on the way and, uh, they're—they just called back and confirmed that they're on their way.

ALAN: Are you the guy from St. Olivia?

PAUL: I'm sorry?

ALAN: Are you—you . . .

PAUL: I—I'm the guy from St. Olivia, yes. (.)

((Phone transferred to Leo))

Paul's words are easy and his voice relaxed. He gives a series of compliments to Alan: "You're doing a very good job for me," "I know it's tough in your position," and "You're doing a great job." He also tries to determine what the atmosphere in the classroom is like. According to Gary, this is effective and appropriate.

> The negotiator is doing a good thing; he's getting intelligence about the hostages without it coming across in a sinister way. . . . In a very nonthreatening and appropriate way [he] asks a nice appropriate question, "You doin' okay? Everybody else okay? Anybody injured in there at all?" Things that even if the subject was listening, he wouldn't take offense at. It wouldn't be obstacles to the rapport building so it is a good thing. (Gary, 23, p. 9)

Paul compliments Alan on the good job he is doing and asks him clear questions about the situation inside the school. Unlike the first exchange with Alan, which Paul hoped would be clandestine, this exchange bears no trace of secrecy.

> At this point, I feel relatively comfortable that *he's* going to allow me to talk to the hostages about *that* sort of thing. I didn't feel *any* animosity about doing that at all. None. I felt—in fact, I felt very confident. (Paul, 17, p. 79)

It is interesting that Paul uses the word *confident* to describe his feeling. The exchange with Alan took place right after Paul learned that Leo has asked to speak to him. He *is* confident. For the first time, he is in the position of being asked for by Leo, instead of having to ask for him. Leo's request for Paul shows he has taken Paul up on his previous offer to come to him as someone who can help. It is a significant moment for Paul, and his confidence is clear in his language and his tone of voice.

Leo returns to the phone and begins complaining about Richard. Leo feels he is in a position to discount Richard to Paul; he tells Paul how much Richard bothered him. This discounting of Richard gives useful information about how Leo perceives his relationship with Paul, as someone working on his behalf. This is the role that Paul had positioned for himself earlier; he offered to help Leo by managing the SWAT officers, whom Leo found bothersome. It is interesting that at this point, it is not the SWAT officers, but another negotiator that Paul has to "manage" on Leo's behalf.

At the end of the exchange, Leo makes a slightly threatening remark. On an implicit level, Leo's statement seems to say, "Take me seriously."

LEO: Yeah.

PAUL: Hi, Leo!

LEO: How's it going?

PAUL: How—how— Fine. How are *you* doing?

LEO: ((Inaudible))

PAUL: What's that?

LEO: It's goin' o—it's goin' okay right now though, but I —I'm *serious*, (.hhh) that FBI guy is really fuckin' gettin' on my nerves.

PAUL: Okay.

LEO: Okay. 'Cause I don't want him startin' to shoot. He had people—he had people (.hhh) located over here by the, uh, windows and I don't like any of that shit, all right? (.hhh) I don't want anybody to get shot, uh, accidentally, and I wouldn't want that to happen.

It appears that Leo is threatening a student; however, he is not—he is threatening a police officer. The threat is implicit. Leo says he doesn't want anyone to get hurt *accidentally*.

SWAT officers have entered the building through some small, beveled-glass windows in a first-floor classroom, diagonal to Leo's position on the second floor. The officers broke the windows earlier, after Richard's first phone call to Leo. Leo realizes that there are police officers in the same building he is in; he assumes they are there because of Richard.

70   *Chapter Five*

A SWAT officer is inside the classroom with the broken windows. Now, the negotiation team knows that Leo is aware of her presence. From his position upstairs on the second floor, Leo can look down the staircase and see her in the classroom below. The team hears Leo's threat, and they act on it immediately, for two reasons: They want the officer to move so she is safe, and they want to move the officer so that Leo will feel they listened to him.

> See now, as a negotiator, that's important information to get it relayed back to your tactical team. He said, "I can see the guy at the window." So *that's* information negotiators need to make sure gets back to the tactical team. For one thing, especially with him being armed, that puts it, the tactical officer in danger. But *also*, if you can get that person removed from where he can *see* him, then, that's going to give an extra benny to the negotiator. 'Cause he's going to think, "Wow, I told him to get that guy moved and he *did*." (Jane, 15, p. 37)

Once the team informs commanders, the SWAT officer moves out of sight, but retains her position in the classroom. Leo can no longer see her, but she can still see him. She is prepared to shoot him if given the order.

In the next two excerpts, Paul tries to find out if any teachers are in the building. Leo entered the school to shoot a teacher; if more teachers are inside, the team surmises, there is an increased potential for violence.

> I remember Bob or it might have been Richard passing me that note, "Ask if there's any adults in the room." . . . They might just write a note that says "Adult hostages" and question mark, and you'd know to ask, "Are there any adults in there?" . . . You would want to bring that question into the relevant conversation. (Paul, 19, p. 87)

Although a team member has provided the question, it is up to Paul to figure out a smooth way to deliver it. He builds up to it slowly, first trying to find out how many students are still in the room. This talk leads to a brief discussion about the comfort level inside the building, which is hot and stuffy. Notably, Leo is now using the pronoun "we." He has included himself and the hostages in one group; they are together in their discomfort.

> PAUL: Uh, Leo, Leo, I—I—I don't want that to happen either, you kno?w. Um, uh, so I—so I know I've got enough pizzas there, can you (0.1) reconfirm how many people are there that needs pizzas?
>
> LEO: ((sighs))
>
> PAUL: Can you tell me? Since you let some go?
>
> ((Unintelligible conversation. Leo seems exasperated here))
>
> (5.0)

LEO: >We've got about sixty-five people here now< and we might let a couple, uh, because it is getting crowded in here— we might let some, uh, go a couple hours from now. Okay?

In the next exchange, Paul asks if he can give Leo something to consider. He remarks that the discomfort is due to the large number of people in the room: the "more people" Leo has in the room, the "more body heat," and "the hotter it gets." Perhaps anticipating that Paul's next statement will be about letting more hostages go or ending the incident, Leo explains the efforts he's making to keep the students comfortable. "We" have fans in the room, he says, and "we" have people checking on the air conditioner's timer. At that point, Paul takes the opportunity to find out if any more teachers are inside the building.

PAUL: Okay th— Leo . . .

LEO: [[So, drop off those pizzas . . .

PAUL: [[Okay.

LEO: . . . and I want 'em here in about half an hour.

PAUL: Okay.

LEO: ((Unintelligible)) half an hour.

PAUL: B—Leo, Leo, Leo . . .

LEO: What?

PAUL: Let me give you a couple a things to consider there. Uh, I realize that it's hot (.hhh) and everything, and you realize that the more people you have in that room the more body heat you have and the hotter it gets.

LEO: [[Well . . . we've got about seven fans in here so I . . .

PAUL: [[uh, okay, but it's sure gonna get hot=

LEO: =three or four fans in here.

PAUL: Sure.

LEO: WEll, as LOng as the air conditioner's on and you guys don't fuck with th*at*, everything'll be okay.

PAUL: Okay, well, the, okay, yeah, you have to understand something—that those things are on time things that we can't—we can't, uh, readjust. I mean, we don't have any access to them. (hh)

LEO: Hold on one second.

PAUL: Suure.

((Leo talks to the group about the fans and appears to be getting the group's consensus on something.))

PAUL: Leo?

((No answer))

PAUL: Leo?

((Leo ignores Paul and asks a student, "What's your name?"))

LEO: Okay.

PAUL: Leo?

LEO: Yeah.

PAUL: Okay, good. Uh . . .

LEO: I have some people, we, uh, I have some people [[checking on the timer, uh, we have a coupla people probly know something about it . . . (.hhh)

PAUL: [[Okay, let's . . .

LEO: . . . checking on the timer to see if we can get . . . a little . . . stay on it.

PAUL: Okay, so, so I can help you a little bit here, uh, are there *any ADU*lts there that know about the timers?

LEO: Huh?

PAUL: A—any adults that know about the timers.

LEO: There's no adults in here.

PAUL: Oh, okay.

LEO: No adults that are—all the teachers are out.

PAUL: Oh, okay. Well, I—I was just wondering 'cause sometimes they know a little bit more about 'em than students do. Um, is everything comfortable right now?

In the next sentence, Leo says that because it is uncomfortable inside the building, he is considering moving the students to another room. Paul does not want this to happen, but does not say so directly. Instead, Paul takes Leo's remark as an opportunity to suggest that Leo consider ending the incident. First, he tells Leo that the team is trying to make him "comfortable" and they are working on "the problem" of the heat. Then, he offers "another option" for Leo. He offers to work on this "problem" *directly*.

LEO: Uhh—Everything's comfortable now but, uh, (.hhh) (hh) it is getting kinda hot in here. If it gets maybe a little hotter we'll (.hhh) I'll transfer over to another bigger room. (.hhh) But uh . . .

PAUL: Well, the—the—the problem—the problem—the problem that ya ha::ve is, uh, is that that the air, y'know, obviously is getting—getting hotter in the whole upstairs there and, uh, (hh) so what we wanna do is try to make you as comfortable as possible. We're working on that problem.

Um, there is another option that we can uh *do* and that's just to try to *end* this problem and try to work with you directly. And bel*ie*ve me, I—I'll *do* that. *You* won't be hurt, if you just consider coming out, and *I'll* meet you there and *I'll* talk with you and we'll try to solve this problem together.

In the second paragraph of his statement, Paul rhythmically repeats "we," "you," and "I" in a few short phrases. Also, in the last sentence of the exchange, Paul talks about the end of the incident not with new language (e.g., "surrender" or "give up") but with the same language used before (e.g., "solving a problem").

According to Gary, Paul is planting a seed with Leo that the incident can still be solved. This is different from making an effort to solve Leo's *life* problems, which is what Paul had tried to do earlier.

He is throwing out for consideration, which a negotiator should do fairly early, "You could always come out and you will be treated with dignity," and it's good to plant that seed. . . . There's a subtle difference between that and a negotiator dwelling on problem solving too soon. Problem solving would be "Don't worry about the fact that you didn't get a job; I can help you find a job or you know you can take courses because of the college education you didn't get" and that's trying to solve this person's problems when what is really needed is to understand his emotional response to those problems. . . . We tell negotiators, don't be afraid to fairly early on let the subject know that he can always come out and we will treat him fairly and with dignity. That is a different thing than saying, okay, what I have do is come up with this brilliant strategy to solve his problem and then he'll want to come out. That's a little different. (Gary, 26, p. 10)

In the next excerpt, the seed Paul has planted generates a new discussion. Leo unexpectedly asks how much time he will serve for what he has done. For Bob, it is a memorable moment.

That was Paul's clue that we could talk about it. All of a sudden we can talk about it. It gives you more hope. "I'm not gonna spend the rest of my life in prison." I remember all of us at the same time saying he'll *talk* to us about it. (Bob, 18, p. 49)

Paul attends to the comment's significance in an interesting way. Rather than automatically discussing it, he asks *permission* to discuss it.

LEO: Yeah, I know I'll probably get five to ten years or anything more, right? That's one thing I, we have to discuss. I'm not f*uc*kin' gonna spend the rest of my life in prison.

PAUL: Okay, will you ta:::lk to me about that now?

By asking permission to have the discussion, Paul demonstrates respect, consideration, and interest in knowing when Leo is ready to talk about this important issue. Conveying respect, consideration, and interest will further facilitate the relationship and move the negotiation forward. The progress is evident in the next sentence, when Leo offers a time he will be ready to talk. Also, the phrase "five to ten years" used by Leo in this exchange will be used by Paul at a later point.

LEO: I'll talk to y— ((changes intonation)) I'll talk to you about it after the pizzas get here. How 'bout that, okay?

PAUL: Okay.

LEO: ((silence))

Paul next asks Leo to promise he will speak on the phone again. Up to this point in the talk, he has refused to come to the phone many times. Now, Leo says he will return to the phone, but then briefly becomes agitated, repeating some threats. Then, curiously, Leo changes both his tone and his words. In a softer voice, he says he doesn't want to get hurt. Then, for the first time, he comments on the intentions regarding his behavior.

PAUL: Will you PRomise me that you'll come back on the line and talk to me?

LEO: Yeah. A:::fter the pizzas are here and after, uh, if I don't see no more *SWAT*. But if I see any *SWATs* or SP or FBI, uh, agents, uh, flyin' around or stickin' their, uh, their sniper rifles in here >things are gonna happen, okay<.

PAUL: Oh, well, I understand that, an' I—an' I told you that I would=

LEO: =actually I don't wanna really get hurt . . .

PAUL: Hey, I—I appreciate that and I you know Leo . . .

LEO: I'm just tryin' to make a point.

PAUL: Sure.

LEO: Hey, I didn't—didn't mean ta (0.1) to shoot those people. I—I didn't . . . if I wanted to kill 'em, I woulda killed 'em, all right?

PAUL: I—I know.

LEO: But I didn't. I maimed 'em (.) or I tried to maim 'em, okay?

According to Gary, Leo is minimizing his behavior. Minimization is one of the techniques negotiators typically use. In this case, Leo does the minimization himself. It is one less task for the team; all they need do is build on what he says. They capitalize on this very statement later, affirming to Leo that people are only injured, not dead.

Leo's minimization is helpful for another reason, as it reveals something of how he views himself and his behavior.

> He said, "If I wanted to kill 'em, I would have killed them," and he says, "But I didn't, I maimed 'em or I tried to maim them." Okay, that is a minimization right in one sentence. He makes a very declarative statement. It's almost that he's trying to suggest to somebody that he's not as bad as they would think or, you know, in his mind, "I only tried to maim them I didn't try to kill them." To him that's a lesser responsibility; it suggests to me that he looks at himself as not being that bad. He's trying to convey that to the negotiator. I didn't murder these people. I may have tried to maim them. For most people hearing that, they're saying, What the hell's the difference? But he's trying to use it as a measurement of evilness or culpability. (Gary, 27, p. 11)

The team does not know if Leo believes that no one has died, if he is lying to prepare a legal defense, or if he refuses to believe what he did. But for Gary, these things do not matter. Rather, the team must attend to the fact that Leo's words convey that he is thinking about his future. It is not necessary to know if he is telling the truth.

> It doesn't matter. The fact that he's vocalizing it I view as a good thing because it's almost a precursor to hearing that would lead me to believe that it's almost like somebody that says, "What kind of sentence will I face?" The fact that you posed the question betrays your mind is considering your options. So the fact that you're coming up with excuses or rationales for having done something can almost be looked at in a similar way. (Gary, p. 11)

Gary's comment reflects his understanding that the content of Leo's words reveals something about what he is thinking. The negotiators do not need to know whether or not the statement is true; they only need to attend to the relational aspect of the statement. That is, Leo is interested in discussing possibilities. He is curious.

The team, however, does not attend to the relational feature of the comment. Instead, they focus solely on the content of the statement. In their view, maintaining control of information is the only way to preserve their relationship with Leo. They become anxious about how to keep the fact that people are dead out of Leo's awareness.

> Well, we had to cut the cable. I went to the lieutenant and I said, Look, before we get any further, if there's any cable in the building let's cut it. The news, the

local radio stations are talking about it, let's have a radio blackout so if he can't get any of the information, and that worked to our benefit. (Don, p. 13)

We told the command post that whoever's doing the press releases, that first of all to make sure that you have *control* of the information that's going out to the public. That you have one person as your press officer. And so we relayed information to the command post that whoever this press person is, you need to *play* down the injured and you need to not confirm there's any dead if there's any dead. Like I say, I don't remember how far into it, or if at what point we—we *assumed* there *were* a couple dead anyway, but I don't remember if we were ever confirmed with any information. And if so, at what point into it that we knew. (Jane, 19, p. 38)

We talked about, we were concerned and we sent messages out about trying to assure, we had to coordinate that the news media *didn't* broadcast the fact that anybody was dead. Because that was gonna be our ace in the hole. As a negotiator, one of the things when people are injured or something like that, you . . . say, "Look, you haven't really hurt anybody yet, you know. Yeah, they're shot, but you know, they're still in the hospital, you know. Hey, it's not as bad as it seems." And that was our whole thing. (Bob, p. 16)

Collectively, the team decides not to admit to Leo that anyone is dead. Paul, however, decides on his own that he will admit that Mr. Grant is dead, if necessary. He feels that he has a strong enough relationship with Leo that he can do this.

And I think the consensus of the group was we never admit—we never admit anybody died. I knew in myself, if I was on that line, and he nailed me about Grant, I'd admit it. I knew that. And I *knew* I was gonna go against everybody in that room. . . . But I knew, I felt I had enough rapport with this guy that I could overcome any of the negativity and I could—I could *diminish* any of the, you know, yeah, complicated things, but I could diminish it. (Paul, 20, p. 95)

It is interesting that Paul does not share his feelings with the team. Paul, at this point, has a stronger sense of his bond with Leo than he does with the team, and he is more concerned about attending to the former than the latter. This shift between Paul and the team will not be evident in the text. However, it is evident in the process of how they manage the information about the deaths. At this point, Paul thinks he will be honest with Leo about the death of the teacher. By the end of the negotiation, though, Paul will change his mind and tell Leo no one has died, not even Mr. Grant.

Although the bodies of his victims are right below him, Leo never attempts to go to the first floor to see if anyone is dead. He is not able to do this because SWAT officers are on the first floor. However, many of the student lookouts are walking up and down the stairs, and some of them know about the deaths. Yet, Leo never asks the students about this. Ellen explained why she thought Leo didn't check the status of the people he had shot:

> I guess Paul had him believing that, Hey, it's okay. It could be a lot worse and nobody's killed. And he *believed* Paul instead of questioning the students. (Ellen, 13, p. 17)

At this point, the team is prepared to lie about the deaths, but Paul is prepared to tell the truth about Mr. Grant's death. Yet in the next exchange, the negotiation will go in a different direction.

> PAUL: Yes, we—we know that and you don't know, Leo (.) you don't know how much I app*reci*ate you talking to me because you have h*elp*ed me so much in trying to help *you* that, uh, you know, all of these things that you have done for us has just been outstanding the—the people out here that have come out of the building have told us that you've treated them extr*e::mely* well and we appreciate that and you don't know HOw much we appreciate that and we're willing to go a lo::ng way to help you out because you've helped us.

Paul attends to Leo's view of himself, using words such as "outstanding," "appreciate," and "extremely well." Gary commented that by complimenting Leo, the team is effectively using subtle techniques of suggestion:

> He's trying to convey to the subject that, We're holding you in high regard, you've done some good things, people are coming out and telling us what a great job you've done and we really appreciate the help. What we're basically doing is, it's like a little kid that we reward for some behavior; we're trying to enhance that so that he repeats the behavior. He's being suggestive to him to continue these nice things. (Gary, 28, p. 12)

The twenty hostages Leo released earlier do seem fine. However, the team is not aware of their condition; they have no contact with the students. "We hadn't talked to any of 'em. They whisked 'em away. We never *saw* 'em." (Bob, 19, p. 51)

In the next excerpt, Paul skillfully attends to keeping some content absent from the discourse. He compliments Leo, and this is disconcerting to Leo; he does not know how to answer. He repeats his earlier demands for a television, which is a concern for the team; they do not want to discuss it. Through omission, Paul tries to avoid discussion of the television.

> It was one of those demands, Okay, I'm not going to give it, but I'm not going to tell you I'm not going to give it to you. I'm just going to shine it. And that's what I did, shined it on. Just let it pass. Wasn't going to bring it up again, wasn't

going to, you know, make it important; had *he* brought it up again, we'd deal with it. . . . If I brought it up again, then it'd become *real* important, and I probably would have had to supply it. And I *didn't* want him watching TV. (Paul, 22, p. 98)

Leo notices Paul's omission and comments on it, but instead of pursuing the issue further, Paul agrees that he will try to "work on it." It is a credit to the relationship that this issue does not detract from the conversation between Paul and Leo.

LEO: Okay, and I also want, uh, my request—I want a television in here that'll *work*, all right? Cause, uh, >we're having a problem with one in this one about, something wrong with the, uh, with< the hookup, the cable, so I wanna, uh, black-and-white probably, uh, one with the (antenna) portable one in here and I want it brung in with the pizzas, all right?

PAUL: Okay, well, okay, let— I—I understand that, but do you understand that inside a building with the, uh . . .

LEO: Yeah, but the reception in here's real— ((To a hostage: "Isn't the reception in here pretty good?"))

HOSTAGE: Yeah.

PAUL: Well, not inside the building is the problem.

LEO: Yeah, well, I—I used to go to this school. I know the reception is okay on the top-level floors and I know that there's—there's no interference, so, uh, all right, so . . .

PAUL: I'll—I'll work on that Leo=

LEO: =All right.

The next sentence is a request from Paul to discuss further matters with Leo.

PAUL: Can—can I talk to you just a little bit more about a *couple other things*?

LEO: What's that?

PAUL: Umm, well, you know eve*ntu*ally we wanna end this thing. I—I think that's what I'm hearing from you, uh, is that correct? We wanna end this thing peaceably. *You* wanna get a message across to—right?

LEO: Yeah.

PAUL: Okay. (hh)

Several times now, Paul has qualified his requests with a remark that asks permission. This is a pattern to his questioning approach with Leo. In this case, Paul asks permission to have a specific discussion with Leo. Leo does not agree or disagree, but asks, "What's that?" It is an answer that shows he is interested.

Paul summarily restates key ideas previously addressed in the negotiation. He attributes each idea to Leo—Leo wants to end the incident, he wants to do so peacefully, and he has a message to share. Using the phrase "we wanna end this thing peaceably," Paul paces the summary with Leo. Leo agrees.

The timing and delivery of this agreement was not lost on Gary. It shows how much progress has been made in the negotiation.

> Absolutely first rate. Just a wonderful job as a negotiator. "And can I talk to you about a couple more things?" "Well what's that?" "Well we basically want to end this thing." And he makes the subject agree with him. He said, "Isn't that right? I mean, I think what I'm hearing from you is again, eventually we want to end this thing and that's what I'm hearing from you, is that correct? We wanna end this thing peacefully. You wanna get a message across, right?" And he goes, "Yeah." (Gary, 29, p. 12)

Gary further noted that given the reason for the talk in the first place, the fact that the hostage taker agrees he wants to end the incident peacefully and that he believes he has a message to share is a remarkable shift.

> Right now, this young man probably doesn't know what the hell he wants. He came in the school today based on anger and rage, [but he] probably does not have a clear-cut goal. Does he really expect to get his high school diploma and get his job back and go on and live happily ever after? No. He probably didn't think that far in advance. What he thought about was just fulfilling his anger, and getting his gun, and going to that school and making somebody pay for the injustice that happened to him. So he probably does not have in his mind clearly what he intends to do. He may be suicidal. May not. But I think where this will end is an open question. So now the negotiator, what he's doing consciously or unconsciously is suggesting a suitable ending.... And I think it's really a powerful thing. (Gary, 29, p. 12)

Recall that earlier in the negotiation Paul was able to increase Leo's view of his choices. He did this so that Leo could make a "mental shift" and conceive of alternative ways to end the incident. Now we see that Paul establishes with Leo that the end of the incident is an "open question," as Gary observed. The moment signifies Paul's achievement in introducing an alternative end to the incident, and also, an opportunity to do so.

In the next sentence, Paul does not introduce an end. Rather, he focuses on learning more about Leo's message by asking what Leo wants to say to reporters. This effort fits with what Paul has previously done in portraying himself as a consultant for Leo. So far, he has consulted for Leo with regard to the SWAT officers and Richard. Now, he offers to consult with reporters, someone Leo wants to deal with.

> PAUL: I'd like to talk to you a little bit about that m*ess*age because, umm, you know, o' course the, uh, camera people and all those people are a li::??ttle bit scared to go into a building with a guy with a gun, you know. You could understand that?
>
> LEO: ((Silence))
>
> PAUL: Can't you understand that?
>
> LEO: (.) Well to a point, but . . .
>
> PAUL: Okay—
>
> LEO: THey—THey—THey know how I treated the other guys. They shouldn't have no problem coming in here. [[I'm not gonna kill anybody—unless I'm provoked.
>
> PAUL: [[Okay.
>
> LEO: And if I'm provoked >there's gonna—gonna be a lot of people (.) I—I hate to say the word, but there's gonna be a lot of dead people in here<. Now, I—I hate that word, okay?
>
> PAUL: Okay.
>
> LEO: I really hate it. I just *don*'t want no fuckin' around, okay? And I want everything to be on a truth basis. (hh) I don't want no fuckin' shit started up, okay?
>
> PAUL: 'Kay. Well, you know—you know what I—what I'm hearing from you is that you're an ext*rem*ely sensitive guy. You *don't* wanna see even the smallest animal hurt. You're the type of guy that—that wants to get a message out to people and you wanna *do* it, uh, as peacefully as you can, and we do, too. Okay?

At first, Leo tries to find a way to deal with the reporters himself; he asserts he will treat them well. Treating people well is a theme Paul introduced earlier, with regard to how Leo dealt with the hostages. Paul said that Leo had treated them well. It is a sign of progress that Leo is now using Paul's language to refer to the reporters.

Paul's remarks serve to make Leo appear benevolent. Leo's response to this is to make another implicit threat. He says he won't hurt the reporters unless he is provoked. Paul chooses to focus on the benevolence when he addresses Leo's comments. He says that Leo is a sensitive person who does not want to be hurt or to hurt anyone else. In addressing this theme, Paul folds in some of the same language he has been using throughout the negotiation, about Leo's interest in getting "a message" out in a "peaceful" manner.

Again Paul talks about the incident ending peacefully. His talk includes, rather than excludes, Leo's active participation in the process. The fact that the team can insist on Leo's participation is likely due to something the team achieved earlier. They elicited Leo's commitment to negotiate with Paul. By committing to the negotiation and explaining that he has something to share, Leo has implicitly enlisted the team as his advocate. Leo now needs the team to maintain the view he has constructed of himself with them, as a person with an important message to share.

> PAUL: And so I'm tryin' to work with you here. That's why I need to talk to you as much as po::ssible. So that *I* get the message directly from *you* so that I don't we don't ge::t anything fouled up. Because, uh, you know, sometimes if you put somebody else on the air?? uh, here to talk to us, we don't get, uh, exactly what you're telling us. And it's hard to hear you when you're away from the phone. Okay? (0.2) You understand?
>
> LEO: Yeah, I understand, but when I—when I have something to say I'll—I'll, ah, pick up the phone or (.) All right?
>
> PAUL: Okay, but do you unner— Leo, uh, also you know you have to realize that we sometimes have to give *you* information such as the helicopter and (.) things like that.
>
> LEO: Yeah.
>
> PAUL: And it's *hard* we—we—we aren't getting the communication across to you, okay? And that's why we need to talk to you directly=
>
> LEO: =hold on, all right?

Interestingly, this exchange continues with the theme that Leo is an important person. His importance takes on a broader definition in the next excerpt: He increases the range of *his* role in the incident. Recall that he is something of a helper to Paul. In the next exchange, we see an indicator of this. Leo's comments illustrate how he sees himself in relation to the students—as *their* liaison to the outside.

> HOSTAGE: Tell him aspirin.
>
> LEO [to hostage]: How many aspirin?
>
> LEO: And I also want one, uh, thing of aspirin. We have a couple a people up here with some headaches.

82   *Chapter Five*

> PAUL: Headaches=
>
> LEO: =Yeah and (.) understandable.

Leo asks for aspirin, pauses, and says one word: "Understandable." By asking for aspirin for the students and acknowledging that it makes sense that they have headaches, Leo is empathizing with them and taking care of them. Further, as Jane observed, he is now a "leader" among them (p. 40). Similarly, Leo's concern about the students' welfare gives useful information to the team about who he is *not* upset at:

> See, it's interesting—here you've got a guy that's holding a bunch of people that he's threatening to kill, and now he's trying to get aspirin for their headaches, and he's ordering pizza and stuff for them. . . . I can already sense from listening to this that his anger is not towards those students. He's only made sort of veiled threats that are directed at . . . keeping his security, I mean, "If anybody comes up here I'm gonna kill people." But there hasn't been any threats directly against the students, [that are] unrelated to his defense and security [and] that's an important thing. If there were people in there, for whatever reason, that he was angry at, it would . . . put them in far greater danger than people merely being used as pawns or defensive shields. In this case, he's using them as defensive shields. Now if his former girlfriend is in there, who's jilted him, if it's one of his teachers, if it's someone that's insulted him in school, these people would be at risk. From the interaction that he's having with the hostages that comes out in the dialogue of the negotiations, there is none of that, and that's a good thing. (Gary, 32, p. 14)

In the next excerpt, Paul tries to stall Leo's request for aspirin. The stalling technique does not work. Leo begins to breathe heavily, and he seems agitated. He makes further demands, about coke, pizza, and the television. Now he attributes the demands to the group, not just himself. However, the agitation does not last long. Leo qualifies his statement by telling Paul he trusts him. He subtly suggests that Paul should behave accordingly, as someone worthy of Leo's trust. Paul's response is to explain the ways he has been trustworthy.

> LEO: And uh . . . and I want that brought along with the tee—television, the pizzas, . . . okay?
>
> PAUL: Uh, uh, what—what type of aspirin do you want?
>
> LEO: We want one big bottle of Advil, we want the pizzas, we want the coke, and we want the television. (.hhh) We want it all at one time. (.hhh) We're gonna have two people come down there. (hh) We're gonna have 'em bring it back up here, all right? (.hhh) You're gonna have your men set it down here and we're—we're gonna transfer it back up. (.hhh) There's not gonna be anything . . .

PAUL: Will—will I=

LEO: =You know I'm *trusting you* to this point, so I don't wanna mo*n*key business going on while those pizzas are going up. And *I'm* not gonna eat any of the pizzas, so don't think about drugging it or doing anything to the coke, okay?

PAUL: W—we—we don't work that way, Leo, and I've—I have so far done everything you've asked me to do? and I've let you know about things (0.1) such as the helicopter and, uh, that sort of thing.

LEO: Okay.

PAUL: Um, you know, uh, there's a couple of things that—that I'd like to talk to you about if you have a minute, uh, in reference to, uh, helping you out with the problem with your school and things like that. (.hhh) I've been looking into a couple of programs, uh, while I was off taking a break here. Um, Port College has a *pro*gram that helps out with, uh, uh, where—where students haven't passed their high school. (.hhh) They have a program there that will help you get the, uh, your high school dip*lo*ma. You can actually, uh, transfer the units from the college back to Jefferson High? and . . . Go on . . .

LEO: Yeah, can—can—can I ask you a question about that?

PAUL: Sure.

LEO: If—if, uh, if I did do that, what about the time I'm gonna be serving, 'cause I know I'm not gonna be slapped on the wrist and go straight to Port Coll??ege ((voice cracks on *college*)), all right?

Paul introduces a specific solution to address Leo's learning disability; he knows about a program for kids who haven't graduated high school. Leo's response is skeptical. Yet the fact that Leo responds indicates that he is weighing his options and considering his alternatives:

> [Paul] said there are some programs out there. And instead of the subject saying, "I'm not interested in those damn programs. You're lying to me," what does he say? "Well if I did that . . ." Ding! . . . "You know, what about the time I'm gonna serve?" He's already beginning to explore in his mind that he has options other than killing himself. That's a very critical thing. The fact that he's responding and asking a question that expands on the information, or furthers that line of thought, is a positive thing. [If he] slammed the door shut on it, it's not a good thing. But he, "If I did that . . . ," you know, it shows he's interested. He's thinking about it, he's weighing options. That's what a negotiator wants. (Gary, 34, p. 16)

The team now knows that Leo expects to serve time in prison. They decide that they are going to tell him he is right.

Once he—he acknowledges, I'm not going to *get* a slap on the wrist, I'm going to go to prison, we have a pretty big discussion after we get done with that particular, you know, on our break. And we come to the determination that in fact we're going to acknowledge the fact he's going to do some time. (Paul, 26, p. 100)

At this point, Leo's tone of voice is very low and quiet. Several hours have passed, and the team is certain he is tired. They hear fatigue in his voice. Further, he seems tired of dealing with the young hostages:

All of a sudden you have these rug rats, getting on his nerves. There was no doubt they were getting on his nerves. They *were* getting on his nerves. Because my recollection is, "Hey, hey, don't do that!" He'd be telling them don't do that. He'd tell them to sit down. You know, and he, he'd ignore them! ((Laughter)) (Bob, p. 24)

The changes in Leo's talk and the fact that he acknowledges he knows he will go to prison are cues that greatly influence the remainder of the discourse. Concerned that Leo is suicidal, the team spends the rest of their effort conducting a crisis intervention. They assertively work to end the incident by offering Leo a written agreement regarding his prison sentence. Further, they use specific language to get him to visualize a suitable, safe, and believable end to the incident.

The team's final efforts are crystallized after a consultation with crisis negotiators at the FBI Academy in the Special Operations and Research Unit (SOARU—the Crisis Negotiation Unit that exists today was not its own entity at the time). Negotiators at the SOARU have produced a "psychological profile" of Leo, based on information from the Jefferson team. Essentially, the profile is a cursory personality assessment, derived from data about the incident and the negotiation effort thus far. It includes ideas for how the negotiators should proceed.

Bob Bixby was the one that, about, I'd say about six thirty, seven—he was always trying to get me alone, saying, Hey, come on, we've got to talk, we've got to talk—finally got me alone and said, Okay, now this is what I've done, I've called Quantico and here's the personal profile, and he laid it all out for me. (Paul, p. 22)

Once [Bob] gave me the outline of what I should be doing, it was straight down the pike from there. (Paul, 08, p. 55)

Bob has taken it upon himself to phone the negotiation unit at the Academy. He spoke to one of his old instructors, Clint Van Zandt, whose suggestions have immediate fit for Bob. The team is already doing some of what Van Zandt suggests.

[Van Zandt] said, "Since you got him to this point, here's what you say to him, if you haven't said this already . . . ," and we had said most of them. Like, *when* you come out. Start out, not *if* you come out, start with when. (Bob, pp. 24–25)

Van Zandt even has a prediction for Bob about the end of the incident:

I gave him the whole scenario, gave Clint the whole scenario, and he said, "Well, it sounds like you're doing exactly the right thing," and I said, "Well, now we got to get him out." "Well," he said, "he'll come out." He said, "I'm sure he'll come out." (Bob, p. 25)

The conviction with which Van Zandt predicts the inevitable surrender makes an impression on Bob. He takes the suggestions back to the team with confidence.

Well, yeah, I felt good, and I think I went back in and I think I told Paul—I said, well, we're doing exactly what's right. So I say, "Here's some of the terminology" and I had those things written down, and he started using them, and we started using them, and then it just kind of . . . like out of a textbook, like it's coming out of a textbook, everything I'd ever *read*, everything I'd ever *done*. (Bob, p. 25)

The specifics of the consultation with Van Zandt deal with how the team should talk to Leo. They are to focus on eliciting comments from Leo about how he wants to end the incident. According to Van Zandt, Leo is now at the point where he wants to surrender.

After I told Clint what had progressed, he said he's at the point *now*, that he wants to come out. Now you have to get him. You start saying *when* you come out, *start* harping on, you know, about *how* he's gonna come out, and *what's* gonna happen, and he said that's—you're at that point *now*. And so that's where I went back in and we discussed it, and that's when [Paul] just said, you know, let's talk about coming out. (Bob, 33, p. 56)

The profile gives Paul confidence. The experience and seasoning of the people who put it together convince him of its utility. It helps him synthesize in his mind how to organize his approach.

It was the first time that the validation came that these guys really knew what they were doing. . . . They've been there, they've done that, I mean, these people have worked this type of things for years. They had the experience I lacked. I had the technique, I had the ability—I didn't have the experience to draw from to put all this stuff together. The pieces of the puzzle. And that's where they came in and really saved the day. No doubt about that. (Paul, p. 23)

86   *Chapter Five*

Team members also sense the significance of the profile. Don places its importance on the same level with the information learned from Leo's family members at the scene.

> [The] profile, I think, was invaluable. Because for the most part it was very correct, 'cause we didn't really know who or what we were dealing with. In talking to his mother and, I think, and his brother—they were both at the school . . . what type of person are we talking about. What are we dealing with here, what type of person, emotionally, physically . . . what do we know about him? Where do we not go? What buttons do we not touch? Tell me about it. That was invaluable. (Don, pp. 67–68)

Several other key events take place between the third excerpt at 6:15 P.M. and the fourth one at 8:30 P.M. At 6:30, Paul talks to Leo about what his life in prison can be like—that it may be a way to better himself. Leo says he will talk about this only after the pizzas are delivered. The delivery takes place at about 7:00; Leo lets another twenty students leave the building afterward.

At about 7:30, Leo hears a news report on the hostage taking. The reporter gives Leo's actual name as Lewis Johnson. He is described as a disgruntled ex-student who went on a shooting rampage at his former high school. When Lewis confronts Paul about having known his real name all along, Paul says he wanted to wait until Lewis was ready to give the name himself.

At 6:40, the hostage taker lets Alan call the negotiators to ask if they will call Alan's parents and let them know he is okay. Paul takes this request as an opportunity to get the names of *all* the hostages, so he can call *all* their parents. The hostage taker agrees and a list is made.

In the next excerpt, Lewis reverts to stating previous demands. He repeats his request for a reporter. The team is expecting this renewed request; they have planned to offer Lewis a tape recorder instead.

Chapter Six

The 4th Moment: 8:30 P.M.

In the next excerpt, Paul skillfully handles Lewis's request for reporters to talk to, so that he can tell his story to the world.

PAUL: Lewis? Hey how ya doin', Lewis?

LEWIS: Yeah.

PAUL: Okay. Listen, I've got the Advil down here and we—

LEWIS: And you wanna negotiate how many people get out and when. (.) >It's not gonna work<. (.hhh) I said I would send some more people do:w::n when the news guy comes up here . . . (and I respect you guys).

PAUL: Okay. The—the—you have to understand our problem here, okay, and—and, you know, put your place—put yourself in the news guys' place for just a minute. Okay. They they're afraid that they'll get sho::t. 'Kay? And we re— ((loud buzzing noise)) we know *that*—and I know *that*—that's not gonna happen, but I can't convince th*em* of that. What *they* would like to know is that if they sent you a tape recorder would you *tape* record the message?=

LEWIS: =No.

PAUL: I mean, it—it gets out to the same pla??ce.

Paul attributes the idea of the recorder to the reporters. The entire reason it is necessary, Paul says, is due to the reporters' fear, which Paul acknowledges is probably unnecessary. By saying this, Paul connects with Lewis, and that connection allows him to go one step further. He asks Lewis to consider the situation from the reporters' point of view.

The team's offer of a tape recorder is an attempt to find out more about Lewis's message.

What we were doing was trying to figure out what he was going to say to the news people. We wanted to know what he was going to say. That's why we offered to send the tape recorder up there. Why don't you take this tape recorder, talk to the tape recorder. Because it would have given us, we were hoping it was going to give us some clues to what he was going to say. (Paul, 27, p. 101)

According to Gary, this effort is a productive way to get more information:

It's a great way to get him to talk about what is clearly something he wants to do. We're trying to identify what does he want to do in this so-called press conference? He wants to tell it to the press when they come in; he doesn't want to share it with us. And what Paul does, what the negotiator does here, is say, Maybe if you related it to me, I could—I could use it to convince them that they should come in and talk to you. It's beautiful. (Gary, 35, p. 17)

Lewis refuses the recorder. In the next exchange, Paul tries to find out about Lewis's message in another way.

LEWIS: Yeah, but it's in the— >I want—I want some people to understand some—this shit that—and I don't want . . . it happening to more people<.

PAUL: Okay, would you—would you talk to me about *that* for a little bit so *I* understand it and—and, uh, if nothing else maybe I could relate some of that information to the press so that they might be more willing to talk to you. Can we talk about that for a little bit?

LEWIS: (.hhh) We can talk for about—for maybe about five, ten minutes.

PAUL: Okay, that's *great*. Well, 1—let's talk for about five or ten minutes.

Paul offers to relay Lewis's message to the reporters himself and asks Lewis to tell him the message he wants to send. The offer works. Although Lewis does not want a recorder, he does want people to understand all of the "shit" he has had to go through.

Paul asks permission to talk with Lewis a little bit more. The "little bit" turns into a specific amount of time: Lewis, sounding exasperated, agrees to talk for five or ten minutes. Paul's reply to this statement includes an emphasis on and repetition of Lewis's words, something Jane sees as important:

See there again, it's like, oh, okay. You know, he's saying five or ten minutes. I don't know why he would have said that, but by Paul acknowledging, oh, okay, well, we'll talk about it for five or ten minutes, that *again* is like another positive reinforcement: Hey, somebody's listening to me and I have control over this 'cause I told him five or ten minutes and he agreed with it. (Jane, 25, p. 40)

Once Lewis agrees to talk, Paul picks up the conversation as if it is a new phone call.

LEWIS: [[Sure

PAUL: [[Umm, what, uh, tell me again—I mean, obviously you went to school here, right?

LEWIS: Right.

PAUL: Okay, and there were so::me classes that you li:::ked. And got—got through okay.

LEWIS: It's not just that. It's the wa:::y that they—they set up the classes. They set 'em to a—to a—certain people advance and certain people don't get to advance. And the teachers do *not* really—they don't take time with the kids that really need help. A—And I've put up with a lot of sssshhhhit from people here, a lot of other teachers.

PAUL: You know th=

LEWIS: =All right?

PAUL: Lewis, you know that—that's really a shame that you had to do that because, uh, you sound like to me that you're a *very* intelligent individual. And it doesn't seem like they gave you the time (.) to really develop that. And you know, (hhh) God, I—I really hate to see you throw this all away. I think that there's a way that you and I can work this ou:::t, umm, but we can't do it talkin' over the phone. D'you know what I mean?

LEWIS: *Yeah*

Paul asks Lewis to tell him about his school experience. He uses the word "obviously" (without a problem), inquires about Lewis's efforts in other classes, compliments him, and expresses concern that Lewis not throw his life away. The simple sentences sound as if Paul and Lewis are meeting for the first time. Paul seems curious to listen, and Lewis interested to talk. Accordingly, Lewis calmly tells Paul how the situation at the school was a problem for him, a student who needed help. The exchange seems to be about how Lewis did not get what he needed, and the implication is that Paul can give it to him.

Paul's comments sound very sincere and completely believable. I had no doubt, listening to the tape, that he meant what he said. Other negotiators (Patricia, Gary, and Bob) also told me that they thought Paul's genuine interest in getting Lewis out is what made him successful.

> Something that should be said: What probably makes the negotiator successful here is, he's not a good bullshitter, he's probably very sincere. I mean, he's

working very hard toward saving a whole bunch of lives, and I'm sure that he's putting his every bit of his heart and soul into this thing and wants to legitimately give this guy a reason to want to continue on and be positive, so the negotiator, even though he knows deep down the guy's not going to walk away with a happy ending, is certainly not projecting it in his interaction with him. (Gary, 36, p. 18)

Thinking Lewis wants to better himself, perhaps to further his education, Paul discusses some of the opportunities he will have in prison. This issue is important to Lewis, but it will not be addressed until later. At this point, however, it proves useful, as it generates important discourse. Lewis mentions his parents for the first time.

> PAUL: And, if we could work sumpin' out where, you know, we could work on, like, getting you your GED, which is like a high school diploma, they've gotta cla:::ss for that. That you can *take*—you get your high school diploma—that's gonna help you out in the job market. And if you decide to go like to a trade school or—or . . .
>
> LEWIS: It's not just that . . . it's the school . . . it's my parents ((inaudible)) . . . I'm just fed up . . .
>
> PAUL: Tell me about your parents.
>
> LEWIS: What, my mom and my dad?
>
> PAUL: Yeah. Yeah. Tell—tell me about it. You know, they—they have called to find out how you're doin'.
>
> LEWIS: They have?
>
> PAUL: Sure they have. I just—my runner came over and told me that. And, uh, they're concerned about *you*, and, uh, they really wanna see this turn . . .
>
> LEWIS: Yeah . . . (and what . . .)
>
> LEWIS [to hostage]: He's coming right now?
>
> PAUL: Okay, Lewis, anyway, they were—they were concerned that, you know, they want everything to turn out okay. For you. And, uh, they're very, very conce:rned about you=
>
> LEWIS: =okay—but, hold on.
>
> ((Silence))
>
> LEWIS: Hold on.
>
> PAUL: Okay.
>
> ((Silence, static))

PAUL: Lewis, you there?

LEWIS: Yeah, I'm still here. I just had to move the phone. (hh)

PAUL: [[Oh, okay.

LEWIS: [[Okay.

PAUL: Gets a little noisy up there, doesn't it?

LEWIS: Yeah. Especially when ((unintelligible)) in these rooms.

PAUL: ((Laughs, chuckles))

LEWIS: Don't feel like gettin' shot. (hh)

Paul met Lewis's family earlier, along with one of Lewis's teachers, during a break in the negotiation. Now, he can use the information from this meeting in the talk. Lewis is interested in Paul's comments, even moving the telephone in order to hear Paul better. For a brief moment, the two share a small laugh, indicating the comfort level that now exists between them. Moreover, Lewis sounds calm, placid, and interested in listening to Paul. It is a palpable difference in the conversation.

> He's *really* relaxed. He wants to give up now. He just doesn't know how to do it. (Bob, p. 56)

It is the job of the negotiators to tell Lewis how to "give up," as Bob says. With Lewis now open to considering his options, the team can close in on the one they want.

In the next exchange, Paul reassures Lewis that no one is there to shoot him. Then, in a non sequitur, Paul asks Lewis, "Who is Nathan?" It is the first time the name is mentioned. Paul met Nathan during Richard's phone call with Lewis, earlier in the evening.

> [Nathan] was with the parents that night. And I don't know if he was the brother-in-law or good friend or what, but he's the one that said that Lewis broke up with his girlfriend, lost his job, and was upset and blamed Grant for it. [Interviewer: And what made you mention his name or mention him?] Oh, kind of lookin' for another hook. (Paul, 28, p. 102)

PAUL: Yeah, no—well, nobody's out there to do that kind of stuff. Um, (2.0) do you know a guy by the name o' Nathaniel?

LEWIS: Nathaniel who?

PAUL: Huh.

LEWIS: Nathaniel Taft.

PAUL: I'm sorry, Nathan. Nathan.

LEWIS: Yeah.

PAUL: Okay, uh, >who's he?<

The above exchange is another example of using the questioning process as a way to introduce more information into the negotiation system. Paul does not know much about Nathan's role in Lewis's life, but because he posed the question, Lewis knows that Paul has talked to his family and inquired into his life. It leads Lewis to say something apparently unrelated.

LEWIS: Oh, he's one of the—the—oh, you found my letter?

PAUL: Huh?

LEWIS: You found my letter?

PAUL: Your letter?

LEWIS: Yeah, I *left it right there inside my, uh, left drawer*.

PAUL: Where's it at?

LEWIS: Okay, I left it, uh, between my—my bedsheets.

PAUL: Between your bedsheets at home? And there's a letter there? What—what does the letter say?

LEWIS: Uh, just that I'm tired of all the shit and the—the failures and everything and my, uh, my future . . . people and . . . ???

Lewis says he has written a letter and left it in between the sheets of his bed at home. The letter is "kinda like halfway explanation, halfway a goodbye to his mom, and halfway suicide note" (Paul, p. 105). The team does not know about the letter before Lewis mentions it, and they do not ever see it. However, they focus on it in the next bit of dialogue; they also make sure that someone goes to retrieve it.

> It came up during negotiations; I went out, found two detectives, and sent them to the home to do the search. The fruit of that search was the letter. (Don, p. 55)

Lewis appears to have relaxed somewhat by this point, and he is calmer. These are positive indicators of negotiation progress; however, they are also potential indicators of suicidal ideation. Paul, sensing a difference in the talk, is concerned about the latter.

> At this point, things get just a little *hairy* for me because I start hearing this hopeless and helpless tones that you think of in suicide situations and you're

thinking to yourself, Oh, you really don't want this guy to just do himself in front of these kids. I just didn't want to see blood and guts in front of these kids if I could help it. Bottom line. (Paul, 28, p. 102)

Paul's concern is heightened when he notices a difference in Lewis's breathing.

His breath is, you know, just real heavy breathing and, you know, it concerns me at this point because I don't know what that means. It's something *new*. And I basically I'm treating this as this guy's becoming suicidal. I'm going to use some of those skills to keep this guy going. I don't want him to die at this point. (Paul, 29, p. 104)

Paul then introduces someone from Lewis's larger system into the talk—a teacher, Ms. Munroe. Introducing this third party further stabilizes the relationship between Paul and Lewis. The teacher is a source of something positive for Lewis.

PAUL: You know, I—I don't understa::nd *one thing*, uh, Lewis. You know, I—I—I had an opportunity to talk to, uh, one of your teachers, your drama teacher?

LEWIS: Yeah, Ms. *Munroe*.

PAUL: Ms. *Munroe?* And, you know, she told *me* that you were one gi::fted individual when it come to drama. And . . . you know, I mean here's an area that you *ob*viously accelerated in and excelled very well in. You one of the guys—she said that you were one of the guys, that you . . . when the stage is there and, uh, organized things, a very good organizer, and, uh, you were the type of person that that she could *al*ways depend on. Seems like—like, uh, if you were *that* dependable *there*, then, you certainly are dependable in *oth*er areas. And you're very—you're a very articulate young man (.) talking to you here (.) you have a very good vocabulary. It seems like, uh, that there's all kinds of things that you have to look forward to. And, you know, hey, a few mistakes—we've all made 'em.

When Paul mentions Ms. Munroe's view of Lewis, he uses the words "gifted," "accelerated," "excelled," and "organized." Paul also says that the teacher described Lewis as dependable: "Seems like if you were that dependable there, then you certainly are dependable in other areas." Paul uses Ms. Munroe's description to plant an idea with Lewis—that he can be dependable in other situations; he can be relied on. Further, Paul says Lewis is "articulate," with a good vocabulary. Each of these statements conveys to Lewis that he has potential; he has things to look forward to in his life.

Lewis's response is skeptical, having heard a second radio report, indicating that people are in the hospital. He knows he will go to prison. Now, he is concerned about how long he will be there and what it will be like for him. Paul has avoided having this discussion so far. Now, he addresses it.

> LEWIS: It isn't like breaking in and stealing . . . One person's in the hospital and might die?? . . .
>
> PAUL: Hey, Lewis.
>
> LEWIS [to the hostages]: Shut up! Okay? ((Suddenly it's quieter))
>
> PAUL: Lewis? I told you h—that if anything *se*rious happened to those people, I would be the first one to tell you. Okay? And I still intend to *do* that. All right?

Lewis comments on his behavior and its results. He says that what he has done is more than just a few mistakes; it's not like "breaking in and stealing." He mentions the person in the hospital, and when Paul starts to reply, Lewis vividly shushes the hostages. Immediately there is a cessation of background noise. Lewis wants to hear what Paul has to say. Paul's answer is vague, he does not admit or deny the deaths or injuries, saying only that he is the person who will tell Lewis if anything changes.

At this point, it appears that Lewis is a willing participant in negotiating how to end the incident. He is interested, and he is communicating it directly. Jane suggested what Lewis might be thinking at this point:

> It's getting serious. He says this isn't like breaking in and stealing a few things. This is more serious. . . . He realizes that he *did* do something more than just go lift a pack of cigarettes. . . . Even though Paul has *downplayed* a lot of it, he still knows it's *serious*. You know, and now it's like, okay, and we're getting into— and *now* it's like, you guys shut up, I've got—I've got stuff to take care of here!! I got to talk to this guy on the phone, you know, you guys, enough of the noise! (Jane, 29, p. 41)

In the next exchange, Lewis shows interest in the information Paul gives him.

> LEWIS: [[hhhhhh
>
> PAUL: [[Right now, right now, yeah, there's people injured, but, hey, they're being taken care of. They're being taken care of. They should be the *least* of your concern. What concerns *you* right now, or sh::ould concern you right now, is the *opportunity* to get your message out. And I wanna help you do that. Okay? Now (.) ob:::viously somehow this is gonna have to come to the end. And we both— we both know that *eventually* . . .
>
> LEWIS [to others]: Gimme that chair!
>
> PAUL: Huh?
>
> ((Silence))

Paul tells Lewis that people are injured, but they are being taken care of. Lewis then asks a student to give him a chair. It is as if he wants to hear better what Paul has to say. Paul minimizes what Lewis has done. He wants to encourage Lewis in the belief that no one is seriously injured and no one is dead. In deceiving Lewis, Paul realizes he is doing something he was trained not to do.

> I mean, I'm battling what I was trained with to what I knew I had to do. . . . I mean, the thought process was there, they told me not to lie, they told me not to. Be as genuine as you can, you know, all this stuff—ain't gonna work here. Sorry. Nice, nice rule, but this one just went out the window. Because this is gonna work. There was no question in my mind I had to do what I did. (Paul, p. 53)

According to Gary, it is sometimes difficult for negotiators to avoid lying.

> We generally say avoid lying. We don't say—a lot of schools say don't, and it's almost impossible sometimes. You certainly want to not do that, frequently, and the negotiator here has from prior conversations sensed that the subject does not know the full extent of the injuries and when he said, "I'll tell you what their condition is right now, they're just injured," he's purposely lying, but that's okay in this context. As long as he leaves himself some wiggle room. (Gary, p. 19).

Regarding the people Lewis shot, Paul says, "They should be the least of your concern. What concerns you right now, or should concern you right now, is the opportunity to get your message out. And I wanna help you do that. Okay?" Paul repeats the word *concern* three times. He is not conscious of the repetition. Rather, he is aware of a purposeful attempt to change the content of the talk.

> I didn't prethink that. I knew I wanted to switch it. The form of diction I used wasn't really— knew I wanted to use it as a tactic. I wanted to get him away from the *negative* of people being injured or killed because I don't *want* him to think that there's any problem there and get back to something that he and I can control. (Paul, 30, p. 105)

In the next exchange, Paul utilizes language recommended in the profile. He asks Lewis how he wants the incident to end, then reminds Lewis of his previous agreements. Further, Paul paces his summary with Lewis and uses a unique rhythm to emphasize the statements. The combination of techniques is disarming.

PAUL: Lewis, are you there?

(4.0)

LEWIS: Yeah.

PAUL: Lewis? Oh, okay.

LEWIS: Okay.

PAUL: What I was saying— Eventually this is all going to have to come to an end here and I kinda like to get, uh, I'd kinda like to get an idea of how you would like it to come to an end. A *pos*itive e::nd like you've told me. And, uh, (0.1) and I'd like to help you with that.

This statement is the framework of the end of the negotiation. Paul and Lewis discuss what will happen to Lewis after he surrenders. They have several conversations after this excerpt, which revolve around Lewis's prison sentence. These conversations become more urgent after Lewis hears a third radio report at 8:00 P.M. It says that nine people are injured and another is in critical condition. It also says that one person is dead. Lewis asks what will happen if the injured person dies. He does not ask about the person who is reported dead; however, after this report, Lewis appears to the team to be suicidal.

Paul continues to minimize what Lewis has done; he is determined to finish the negotiation any way he can. He manages to get Lewis to state the things he wants while in prison, such as counseling and educational opportunities. He tells Lewis he can learn job skills in prison and implies Lewis will eventually be on probation. When Lewis asks Paul how much time he will serve, Paul, remembering Lewis mentioned the quantity "five to ten years" earlier, tells Lewis he will serve less than five years. Paul says that the five years could actually be reduced to as little as eighteen months.

Paul's effort in the final hour of the negotiation is characterized by momentum to finish the job. He loses his ability to pace himself with Lewis.

I was outrunning Johnson. And several times I had to remind myself, if Bob wasn't reminding me, I had to remind myself slow down, take it easy . . . you know, calm down, take it easy. (Paul, pp. 80–81)

In the next exchange, Paul tries to convince Lewis that the judge will take pity on him because of his youth and his emotional distress.

Chapter Seven

The 5th Moment: 9:40 P.M.

In the final excerpt, Lewis makes an interesting comment about himself as a prison inmate; he says that he does not belong with other people, other people who have done things as "ugly" as what he did that night. By choosing these words, Lewis distances himself from his behavior. Paul attends to this information, promising Lewis he will have a solitary prison cell and will have the opportunity to talk to someone about his problems.

> PAUL: And so they're gonna try to do *every*thing they ca::n to make your life *easy*. Now, you still have to, (hh) you know, pay for what li::ttle bit you've done here. Uh, that's—that's *part* of it. Okay? But while you're pa::ying, they're [[also paying
>
> LEWIS: [[You know—you know, what I could understand is putting me in a—in a *padd*ed cell, but putting with someone else that's just as (.) just as ugly and as worse off as what I do tonight—I think that's wro::ng.
>
> PAUL: Well, they don't always put you in the same cell with people. You know at fi::rst they may keep you apa::rt. And let you ta::lk to someone. And let you work with your problems.
>
> LEWIS [to hostages]: What are you—what are you guys doin'? I want you guys to come up this way here.
>
> (3.0)

Like Lewis, Paul builds distance between Lewis and Lewis's behavior. Specifically, Paul wants to dismiss the serious repercussions of Lewis's earlier deeds. People are dead, and the team knows it. Now, Paul addresses that issue directly. Deciding not to admit Mr. Grant is dead, as he had earlier

98   *Chapter Seven*

planned to do, Paul instead tells Lewis that nobody has died. As Paul deceives Lewis, his voice rises and his tone is higher.

> LEWIS: Okay. Uh, so what were you saying?
>
> PAUL: So what I'm saying is—is that you may get—you may get just a very ligh??t sentence in jail. You may end up doin' some counseling at a counseling center. A::fterwards, you know, nobody—nobody has die??d he??re. Uh, that's all in your favor=
>
> LEWIS: =Not yet.

When Lewis says "not yet," it is unclear whether he is threatening hostages, worrying that the victims might die, or alluding to killing himself. Paul takes the comment as a threat to harm others, so he ignores it. Addressing it, Paul surmises, might serve to inflame Lewis once again. In the next excerpt, Paul further minimizes what Lewis has done.

> PAUL: Okay. Nobody's died here. Every—every indication we get from the hospital, those people are doing *just* fine. And they're *stable* and=
>
> LEWIS: =Yeah, they're tell me this . . . if one of 'em die::s, if that guy die::s, then what happens? See, like, it comes up from, what, ten years to twenty years. I know how it works. Okay?
>
> PAUL: But understand the fact, you know, you're *upset*. They take *that* in consideration. *You've ha::d a lo:::t of stress on your life lately, haven't you?*=
>
> LEWIS: =Yeah.

Paul repeats again that no one has died. He says everyone is "stable." Lewis's response indicates that he expects someone will die; he asks what his sentence will be if the victim in the hospital dies. He poses it as a challenging statement, mentioning the condition of the victims only with regard to prison. Will his sentence go up if one of them dies?

Rather than discuss either topic, Paul reminds Lewis of his previous difficulties. He refers to them as making Lewis "upset." Paul's statement about "upset" is set apart from the others in the exchange, punctuated by a softer tone of voice. Paul wants Lewis to admit that he is upset and under stress. If Lewis agrees to this, it will confirm to Paul that Lewis knows Paul understands him. This comment is especially important to Paul, who is concerned that Lewis is suicidal. It is a precarious moment, and Paul wants to make sure he and Lewis are still connected.

Lewis agrees, Yeah, he has had stress. He is very quiet.

In the next exchange, Paul explains that he is speaking with some credibility; he wants Lewis to believe what he says.

PAUL: Okay. The judge understands that. I, >you know<, I've been a police officer for te::n years. I've gone to court in si::milar situations with you and I've seen judges take a lot of compa::ssion.

Ellen responded with sarcastic disbelief to Paul's comment. However, she understood why he said it.

Yeah, I can hear you saying that. I can almost hear you saying that Paul. . . . He's gonna get up and tell the judge he's a real compassionate guy? He just killed four people. But in these situations, you promise whatever you have to promise to resolve the situation. So no one else is injured or killed. (Ellen, 21, p. 20)

Paul says, "I've gone to court in similar situations with you." When I first heard this, I thought that Paul said "with you" deliberately. However, Paul misspoke; he meant to say he'd been to court in situations *like* Lewis's. In our interview, Paul explained,

Well, I wanted to say "like you."

[Interviewer: "Yeah, but it—but it's like a good—a serendipitous thing because you're *with* him. I'm *with* you. I mean, I don't know if I'm making too much of that, but I thought, well, that's a weird way to say it."]

It was actually just a mis—misstatement on my part because what I was trying to say is, "I've been in situations like this and gone to court in situations like that or like yours" and that's what I was—I was really trying to say there and I was just misspeaking.

[Interviewer: "Well, I would, see I wish, I wonder what he heard if he heard that 'with you.' Because he's so connected to you by now, I think."]

Right. Possibly. (Paul, 34, p. 112)

Paul did not necessarily see, as I did, the potential significance of his misstatement for Lewis. Nor did he attribute any conscious purpose to it. His conscious intent was to change the negative to positive.

In the next excerpt, Paul draws out the themes of the talk thus far—repeating that Lewis has had a "bad rap" and that he only wants to share his message with others. Recall that Paul had used the phrase "bad rap" earlier and Lewis had found fault with it because it contrasted too much with his experience. Here, it goes unnoticed. It is a descriptor that Lewis now accepts. Also, Paul speaks to Lewis as if he has already surrendered. He speaks of the surrender in the past tense. This is a way of eliciting change; Lewis can visualize his role in ending the incident because Paul describes it for him.

100   *Chapter Seven*

At the end of the exchange, Paul says something about himself as the carrier of the message. He wants Lewis to know that his voice as a police officer is one of credibility and experience.

> PAUL: *Especially* after somebody like me gets up and says, look, this guy really had a tough time. He really got a bad rap. And he just kinda lost it a little bit and he—he finally came *out* and, you know, treated everybody fine. And he *really* wanted to work, >you know<, on trying to make everybody sa::fe. And just get his message across, and he wants to do something with his life. And, you know, judges consider that. I've seen it. *Ten years*—I've seen that. That's a lo::ng time and track record, wouldn't you say?
>
> LEWIS: Yeah.
>
> PAUL: Okay? (.)

In the next sentence, Paul turns the helping relationship on its head.

> PAUL: Why don't you—why don't you help me out, Lewis?
>
> LEWIS: [[And how's that?
>
> PAUL: [[Why don't you=
>
> LEWIS: =What's your name again?
>
> PAUL: Paul Baker.
>
> LEWIS: *Paul*.
>
> PAUL: Okay.
>
> LEWIS: Mm-hmm.

Paul asks Lewis to help *him*. Lewis starts to ask how he can help, but before Paul can answer, Lewis interrupts. The interruption is unusual in that it serves to reaffirm the relationship: Lewis asks Paul for his name.

In the final excerpt of the talk, Paul paints Lewis "a picture" (Gary, p. 20) of what will happen next. He asks Lewis to lay down his gun and walk down the stairs. Slowly, he walks Lewis through the steps of coming outside voluntarily. Before he paints this picture, he asks *permission* to paint it. He offers the picture as a suggestion to Lewis.

> PAUL: Why don't you just—why don't you do this? I'm gonna make a suggestion. Okay? *Why don't you lay the gun down. Okay. Lay anything down that would hurt someone*. And just walk down that sa::me staircase that the pizzas came up. Okay? Get this all out here, you know, you're gonna feel *be::tter* about this. You're going to—you're going to be able to *get* your message across, and

you know what? Once you put this be*hi*nd you, you're gonna be able to get on with your life. And I'm gonna *help* you do that.

((End of excerpts))

Paul and Lewis have several more brief conversations after this exchange, having to do with a letter to Lewis from the team. Lewis wants the promises Paul has made (about his sentence and his job and educational opportunities) in writing. According to Bob, the fact that Paul promises things to Lewis is not unusual; what is unusual is that Lewis asks for the promises in writing.

> [The] letter and everything, I mean that was, it was *important*, but it was just something, it was a means to get out. You have that in *every*, almost in every hostage situation. Nobody just walks out, without some type of promise. *He* just happened to want it in a *letter*.... Very seldom does it get reduced to writing, like this guy wanted. (Bob, pp. 57–58)

The letter is a ritual of surrender. It is a way for Lewis to participate in ending the incident. The negotiators understand the significance of this seemingly small event. It is a way for Lewis to finish the incident.

> That's right, yeah. Finish it so [he's] kind of on top. You know, and he gets to walk out. You want to do it the easiest way possible for him and you're—you're really willing to do anything. Just to get him out. To do it himself. That's very important. (Bob, p. 58)

Patricia takes responsibility for coordinating the construction of the letter:

> We got that worked out verbally with him and then I had made some notes about what was going to be agreed to and I would have landed a spaceship on the front lawn for him if he wanted it. Whatever he wanted, that's what we were going to do. So I went out and I didn't trust myself to try to type it up myself, but I dictated it to the same old secretary that was still there and she typed it up and ... it said, "I, under Sheriff Jimmy Drennan, hereby agree that Lewis Johnson will do no more than five years" and that it'll be done in a minimum-security prison that affords him educational and job opportunities. And so he has it in a single cell. It's just a short little thing. (Patricia, p. 8)

The team delivers the letter, and Lewis has the remaining hostages sign it. One student makes copies of the letter, and Lewis gives each a copy prior to releasing them at 10:15 P.M.

At 10:25 P.M., per Paul's instructions, Lewis puts his guns and ammunition in the corner of the classroom, takes off his shirt (to alleviate concern about hidden weapons), and walks down the stairs with his hands over his head. A SWAT team immediately intercepts him at the foot of the stairs, handcuffs him, and deposits him in a police cruiser. He is in custody by 10:30.

SUMMARY OF THE END OF THE INCIDENT

Once Lewis surrenders, the team leaves the negotiation room, where they have been for eight hours. For several, stepping outside the Administration Building is a vivid transitory moment.

> I left that room and went outside. When I went outside, it was like, my God, there were lights and cars and cameras, and people and helicopters, and I had no idea all that was going on out there 'cause I'd been in this little bitty room all this night, so I was absolutely amazed to see all that going on. (Patricia, p. 12)

> I remember I got up and I walked outside and I thought, man, I need to stand up and walk around. And I remember I went into that open office lobby area directly out of the room, and then when I went out of that building, I remembered all I saw were lights and uniforms. They had the—I don't know what they're called, but the big lights that come up off the fire engines, and all I saw was uniforms. Police uniforms, ambulance, fire department—it was just lights and uniforms. (Jane, pp. 28–29)

> When we came out, I was just—I was quite amazed. . . . When I came out of that room and went outside, saw helicopters, ambulances, highway patrol, and county sheriff and city police from Steubenville and St. Olivia, and I mean just everyone was there. . . . The magnitude of this is really what overwhelmed me. (Ellen, p. 23)

As the incident is ending, some team members walk over to the cafeteria to debrief the hostages. Patricia and Don begin to plan how to process the crime scene. First, however, Patricia is determined to see Lewis face to face. When she realizes he is walking down the staircase to surrender, Patricia takes herself to the Arts Building.

> I walked straight over to that entrance, to the Arts Building, and Lewis had just come down the stairs when I got there, and I saw him lay down on the floor and the SWAT team then went up on him and cuffed him up, and I just stood there watching this. Lt. Yrlas was standing right there with me and I believe—I don't know—there were a bunch of people, but I was standing right there in that doorway, and they stood him up and I was like this close to him, as close as you and

I, a couple of feet apart. And I just looked at him in amazement and I thought, He's just a kid, he's just a kid. I couldn't believe it. 'Cause in my mind, you know, I had this big raging bull monster picture—that this had to be a really evil, evil person to have done something like this. And to see this little chubby kid— it was like, how could you have done this? (Patricia, p. 12)

Chapter Eight

Nine Techniques of Effective Crisis Negotiation

Prior to discussing the patterns of effective and ineffective negotiation communication skills utilized in the Jefferson incident, it is important to point out two of the limitations of this research study: The first is that I did not involve Lewis in the study, and the second is that, in the study, I chose to focus on just thirty minutes out of four hours of conversation.

I decided not to include Lewis for several reasons. First, the Jefferson incident is still an active legal matter for him; involving him in this research would have risked potentially adverse effects for his legal situation, as well as potential problems for the study. For example, I could not have interviewed Lewis using IPR, as I could not have taken any recording equipment into his prison. Furthermore, I did not want to interview Lewis unless I had the freedom to ask him direct questions about his participation in the discourse, but answering such questions risked possible harm to his pending appeal. While his rights would have been protected by an attorney, he did not have one assigned to him at the time I conducted the fieldwork.

The second limitation of the work is that it examines only five excerpts (essentially thirty minutes) of a four-hour conversation. Although my method of choosing these excerpts was consistent with a naturalistic approach, by narrowing my focus, I also narrowed what I found. I may have made interpretations I would not have made had I examined the entire negotiation in more depth.

PATTERNS OF EFFECTIVE NEGOTIATION COMMUNICATION

In very specific ways, the team created a productive environment for the discourse to flourish. One of the most effective things they did was to isolate themselves so they could focus on their work. They kept other police officers out of the negotiation room and made no effort to find out what was happening outside at the scene unless it was for a reason. Finally, they all sat down around a table and listened to the talk. The team's isolation and ability to focus is compelling; it was in marked contrast to the rest of the scene.

> Oh, Lord, you talk to the guys that were outside the building; it was very loud, very chaotic, very fast paced—I mean, buses coming and going and people and noise, and people screaming and shouting, and we heard none of that. We were in a bubble. We were in a bubble even more so than the command center because we were in the negotiation room. . . . [I] have no idea what was going on outside. None. I mean, I can imagine. But I didn't know. I didn't see it, I didn't hear it. (Don, p. 70)

The team was so focused on their effort that they did not notice time in the usual sense. In their "bubble," the team had a very different relationship with time than others at the scene. They experienced a kind of time suspension, an indicator of their attention to the discourse process.

> It was amazing how time didn't drag. It wasn't like this is taking forever. It was, look at your watch, it's five o'clock—look at your watch, it's eight thirty. . . . It went fast, it went really fast. It was just bizarre how time passed like that. (Patricia, p. 7)

> Like to me, [time] didn't seem like much of anything. It didn't seem to go by fast, it didn't seem to go by slow, it was just kind of like there and we were plodding along doing our job. But to those parents, you know, that just had to have been an incredible time. That's what a lot of them said afterwards: Well, what took so long? Why'd it take so long? Not understanding the dynamics, you know. (Jane, p. 28)

Although the team had a clear understanding of their role as negotiators conducting discourse, there were times they had to step away from that role to make certain that their work could continue undisturbed. They protected the discourse by minimizing outside interference that could have been detrimental to it. When it was necessary or beneficial to the dialogue, they worked with the larger system of commanders, media, and SWAT officers. The ease of this coordination furthered their effort. They had the freedom and flexibility to remain in their bubble.

> And I think several things contributed to the success of this. And not just the people in this room and not just Paul, and it's kind of a salute to the *department*, is we did not have any interference from the command post. I can tell you, I have been in there where you have—maybe this is particular to the FBI—I don't mind putting it on the tape, because I have told agents-in-charge before that come *in* here, and they *sit* down and they wanna *tell* you what to do, and you almost have to turn around and say, "Look, *your* job is to watch out for the function of all of this. Not to come in here and tell me how to negotiate with this jerk." We had nobody come in, and I have seen this even in real life, I've seen it. We had nobody come in here and say, "Let's get this over with." You know— "Do you know what time it is?" We've had that. We had, you know. [Interviewer: "Is it subtle? Or overt?"] Oh, very overt! And we had *none* of this. None of this. We had *no* interference. We had none of this. (Bob, pp. 31–32)

The team members established an atmosphere that was extremely conducive to the development of the negotiation. They processed the talk as it was ongoing, they discussed their ideas openly, and they focused their attention on what would work best in the context of the situation. Their team process, and the cohesiveness with which they brainstormed ideas, was fundamental to the entire effort.

The Jefferson team's collaborative effort was a major contribution to the success of the discourse. Each team member repeatedly told me how valuable it was that they worked well as a group, discussing their different views in order to facilitate the discourse process. Despite their different backgrounds and lack of experience working together, they generated multiple ideas, creating a cohesive depth of vision about Lewis and their conversation with him. This depth of vision allowed them to develop a rich understanding of his situation and to shape a conversational approach that would be most beneficial to the process.

The team tracked very closely what seemed to be working in the discourse. The most evident example of this had to do with the brief change in negotiators. Once the team realized Lewis did not like Richard and preferred to talk to Paul, they did not waste any time going back to their original strategy. Team members described this approach as getting "back on track" (Ellen) and keeping "track of what seems to be working" (Richard). This ability to be flexible was extremely productive to the discourse.

Paul, as the primary negotiator at Jefferson, was the voice for the team. He flourished in the environment that they created for him as speaker. The team gave Paul feedback, ideas, and support. Their presence, as an attentive audience to the talk, helped him in numerous ways. In turn, however, Paul brought unique skills, techniques, and methods of his own to the discourse effort.

> This is about as good as negotiations get. He does everything so, so very well. ... You take a basically high-risk incident in which there would seem to be no negotiation possibilities, and he literally convinces this person that, hey, you know, there is a future, there's something for me, I can be understood, I can maybe serve a little time and—but get my life back in order, and there's opportunities. Well, to leave someone that impression after what they've just done is pretty creative. But he's done it. He's done it. He's been genuine, he's been sincere, he's projected willingness to help, he's been nonjudgmental, he's provided the guy with rationales and excuses for what he's done, but he hasn't done it in a phony way and he hasn't gone over the top. (Gary, pp. 20–21)

Paul was able to develop, amplify, and manage the discourse because he mastered the most fundamental aspect of negotiation: listening. Paul gave Lewis extraordinary attention, listening to what Lewis said to him. This active listening gave Paul access to information *about* Lewis directly *from* Lewis. He found many ways to use this information, which I will detail below. Certainly listening alone is not sufficient, but without it, Paul would have had nothing to build on.

1. Embracing "Manna from Heaven"

Several team members noted the significance of the early statements Lewis made about his situation with Mr. Grant. Paul, who knew what it felt like not to be understood by a teacher, described this information as a "gift from God" and "Manna from heaven." To take advantage of this gift, Paul used self-disclosure. In a very subtle way, he mentioned his own experience to elicit comments from Lewis. With comments such as, "There's a lot of us that's had a tough time in school. Believe me, I did," and "I had a real tough time in school. So I understand that," Paul spoke generally about his own difficulties as a student. He never said too much about his own experience, but he said enough to allow Lewis to make his own conclusions.

Later, by saying, "It's obvious the teacher didn't understand you," Paul communicated his understanding indirectly. Lewis responded to this comment ironically; he knew Paul understood his situation. Paul's demonstration of understanding in this way served to connect him further to Lewis. It also showed his interest in hearing Lewis's worldview (Vecchi, 2002) and his effort at trying to make sense of Lewis's life.

In the Jefferson negotiation, the team worked hard to gain an understanding of Lewis's situation and the events that precipitated the shooting at the high school. The contextual information they learned gave them ideas and direction about what was important to Lewis, and it was vital to the discourse effort.

> [Paul] started off with, you know, *exactly* what he should have started off: to *let* him talk, to find out *why* he did it, and that's what's going on here. I mean, all of a sudden now we know why—Lewis's relationship with the teacher that he killed. (Bob, 02, p. 42)

2. Staying in Conversation

Paul made many efforts to sustain a conversation with Lewis despite Lewis's attempts to end the talk. An example of this occurred very early in the negotiation. Paul asked for a name to call Lewis and told him it did not matter if the name was real. Paul was not interested in gathering facts; he was interested in developing his relationship with Lewis. Another example occurred when Paul told Lewis he was in an office but he did not know which one. Paul wanted to disconnect himself from the school, a place he associated with Lewis's failed dreams. Paul was trying to join with Lewis by separating himself from the school.

Paul's skillful avoidance of Lewis's demands or questions are worth commenting on, as they were in direct contrast with how Richard responded to Lewis's inquiries. Paul did not ignore Lewis's queries; he always answered them in a way that acknowledged what Lewis asked. Thus, it seemed to go unnoticed that the content of the answer was lacking. Paul gave an answer, which acknowledged the value of Lewis's question, but which did not provide any substantive information. Addressing Lewis's questions in this way further sustained Paul's connection.

3. Looking for "Hooks" and Fishing for Clues

Paul introduced other people from Lewis's life into the conversation as a way to introduce new information into the negotiation system. Discussion of the people in Lewis's larger system—his parents, Ms. Munroe, Nathan—helped to further establish the relationship in two ways. It showed Lewis that Paul had talked to people in his life. It also helped to bring more information to the talk, information that Paul developed as themes in the discourse. Paul described his use of Nathan's name with Lewis as "looking for another hook." The mere mention of Nathan's name resulted in Lewis telling Paul about the suicide note left in his bed.

Similarly, Paul looked for hooks and clues when he told Lewis that his drama teacher, Ms. Munroe, had said he was a dependable person. Paul used this description to compliment Lewis and plant an idea with him that he could be a dependable person in other situations. The team attended to people in Lewis's life as a way to generate more information that might further the negotiation discourse.

4. Becoming "the Guy That Helps"

Paul was able to utilize these people in the talk because he established a wide role for himself as the manager of the conversation, as both a negotiator and a consultant to Lewis. By positioning himself in these ways, he increased his flexibility as a negotiator. He was not just an attentive listener; he was someone who could help manage things for Lewis. This management began as an attempt to deal with the people causing chaos and confusion (SWAT officers, Richard). However, it evolved to include others important to Lewis (reporters, parents, Nathan). Each time Paul introduced new ideas related to his expanding role, he made sure Lewis agreed with him by using another technique, switching, which is discussed below.

Paul's maneuverability was clear in that he could utilize the multiple roles he created for himself as negotiator. These roles were subtle, and they were specific to the conversational process. At different times throughout the talk, Paul was either a sincere listener to Lewis's message, a manager of the "chaos and confusion," or a helper who needed Lewis's cooperation to end the incident.

A particularly creative example of such maneuverability can be seen in Paul's handling of Lewis's request for a news reporter. Paul first suggested Lewis use a tape recorder, rather than a reporter, as a way to share his "message." When Lewis declined, Paul then suggested *he* could tell Lewis's message to reporters. Paul positioned himself as a conduit between Lewis and the media. By offering the tape recorder, then himself, as a messenger, Paul subtly encouraged Lewis to talk more about his life. This introduced new information into the conversation (Boscolo, Cecchin, Hoffman, & Penn, 1987).

Significantly, the Jefferson team coordinated their negotiation discourse with the efforts of the SWAT team. A specific example of this occurred when the team learned Lewis had seen the female sniper. They told commanders that she needed to move, not only so that she would be safe but also so that Lewis would feel that they had listened to him.

5. "Planting Seeds" and Growing Options

Paul made several suggestions to Lewis that he could end the incident peacefully and that he would not be hurt. He planted seeds with Lewis that there were other options available to him. In this way, Paul created more options for Lewis. Accordingly, Lewis asked Paul about the prison sentence he would serve; he wanted to discuss it, and he said so. Several negotiators pointed out Lewis's query as showing that Lewis had begun to consider alternatives to his situation.

The ability to "plant seeds" with someone who feels they have no more choices to make is a very powerful way to introduce change. The subtlety involved is in direct contrast with advice giving, such as telling someone what to do. Rather, planting a seed in fertile ground can help to increase a person's sense of choices and alternatives about his or her situation; this contributes to the likelihood of change.

6. Asking Permission to Ask

Lewis saw himself as a disrespected student who had a message to share and a need to tell his story. Paul attributed value to the message and esteem to Lewis's point of view. Several times, immediately before discussing a topic that Lewis mentioned, Paul first asked Lewis's permission to discuss it. He did not assume he could talk about it right away. This technique conveyed respect for Lewis and curiosity about his story. Furthermore, Paul offered ideas about how Lewis could share his message, and he repeated Lewis's language. These practices implicitly attended to Lewis's need for respect and recognition.

7. Forming "Little Commitments"

Paul used a very effective pacing technique with Lewis that had a clear discernible pattern: Paul made a statement ("Now what I think I'm hearing from you is you wanna end this thing peacefully"), posed a subtle question at the end ("Isn't that right?"), and then after Lewis answered "yeah," confirmed Lewis's agreement ("Okay. Now . . ."). This technique allowed Paul to obtain numerous commitments from Lewis to end the incident peacefully. The repetition of this technique, as well as its consistent use, was further enhanced by Paul's tone of voice. He sounded genuine, sincere, and interested.

8. Switching

In addition to pacing his talk with Lewis, Paul also skillfully paced how he introduced new *ideas* to Lewis. For instance, Paul attended to the ideas of Lewis wanting to "move" to another room and Lewis being "concerned" by using a pattern of pacing and leading. Lewis could still "move," but instead of going to another room, he could end the incident; Lewis could still be "concerned," but about himself, rather than the condition of the victims.

What is consistent about this technique, which Paul called "switching," is that Paul always repeated something that was acceptable about Lewis's idea before he introduced a change to it. Consistently, the variation was in the direction of ending the incident. Paul described this switching process as an attempt to shift the content of the discourse from negative to positive.

The technique of switching Paul used in this negotiation was extremely effective in investing Lewis in the negotiation process, and thus, increasing the choices and options Lewis could make about how to end the negotiation. Paul's technique of planting seeds in order to increase options is evident throughout the discourse. This pattern of switching also kept Paul connected to Lewis in a more subtle way: Lewis often introduced the words Paul later used to introduce change. Also, repeating the idea prior to varying it, Paul made the change appear less dramatic. In this way, Paul planted seeds with Lewis about other options that were available to him.

9. Using the Language of the Hostage Taker

Crisis negotiators have emphasized the significance of silence, pauses, and reflective statements; however, negotiators are typically instructed to refrain from using a hostage taker's language. In fact, the negotiation literature suggests negotiators should try to change hostage takers' language. However, this suggestion primarily refers to inflammatory language; thus, what has evolved in the literature are really techniques for "softening" a hostage taker's language. Negotiators have not written about which parts of the hostage taker's language to keep and which to avoid.

Paul's approach to Lewis suggests negotiators need to make some new distinctions. He skillfully utilized specific aspects of Lewis's language *and* also consciously avoided others. When it was inflammatory, Paul changed Lewis's language (e.g., Lewis: "Don't fuck with me"; Paul: "No one's here to screw with you"); but when it was productive, Paul repeated Lewis's language. Sometimes he did the repetition immediately; for example, when Lewis said, "We can talk for five or ten minutes," Paul quickly repeated, "Great. Let's talk for five or ten minutes." At other times, the repetition came several hours later, such as when Lewis said, "I'll get five to ten years right?" and Paul used "five years" later when he and Lewis discussed Lewis's likely prison sentence.

PATTERNS OF INEFFECTIVE NEGOTIATION COMMUNICATION

There are some things Paul did that were ineffective and served to undermine his relationship to Lewis. Paul undoubtedly noticed these early difficulties in the discourse, given that he was eager to turn over the phone to another negotiator. In fact, Paul was doing better than he thought. However, the things he did poorly shaped his successful effort and warrant further discussion.

Saying "I Understand"

Initially, Paul relied on his own personal connection to Lewis's story as his only guide for the negotiation. He acted as if he did not need an explanation of Lewis's story because he had had a similar experience of his own. This was ineffective. Paul assumed he understood Lewis's experience when he had not yet given Lewis a chance to talk. This led him to claim "I understand" without *demonstrating* that he understood.

Trying to Solve Things Too Quickly

Paul made many premature attempts to end the incident, and this often resulted in Lewis trying to shut down the conversation. Paul's early attempts to do this were overt and direct. In the first phone call, when Lewis was trying to tell his story, Paul was not listening, he was advising: "There are ways that I can help you"; "That's in the past now. What's in the future is what we can do now"; "There are some ways that we can help you with college." These very specific solution attempts were offered too quickly and did not allow Lewis to tell his story. They often resulted in Lewis yelling and cursing at Paul.

Aligning with the SWAT Team

When Lewis asked him who was outside the scene, Paul said, "There's a lot of us." In so doing, Paul aligned himself with the other police at the scene. At this point, he should have begun to distinguish himself from the other police officers. He might have said, "There's a lot of police out there" or "I don't know how many of them are out there." This sort of comment would have set Paul apart from the SWAT officers and conveyed to Lewis that Paul was not one of them. Eventually, Paul did do this. Had he continued to equate himself with the other police, however, it undoubtedly would have been detrimental to the process.

Ignoring Important Markers

Paul lost several opportunities to pick up conversational markers Lewis left for him. For example, Lewis said it wasn't just school problems—that there were other disappointments in his life. Paul, hearing this, offered to come up with a solution before allowing Lewis to talk about these other disappointments. Paul was afraid such a conversation would lead to more problems; however, these markers Lewis mentioned would have been worth listening to.

Interrupting Indiscriminately

In the early part of the negotiation, Paul interrupted Lewis often, and he kept talking when Lewis was trying to interrupt him. Paul told me this was something he realized much later, after he heard himself on the tape.

> You can find places where I'm talking, he's trying to talk . . . you know, I was trying to get my point across, then he wanted to say something. Well, what he . . . says is more important than what I say . . . and I think that's probably just inexperience from not doing this. Where somebody who has done this time and time again, as soon as they hear him start to say something, they shut up. (Paul, p. 61)

Paul's comment indicates the value he found in reviewing his negotiation effort. Listening to himself, he was able to reflect on what he could have done better. Paul wanted to learn from his experience at Jefferson; reviewing the taped discourse was an important and effective means to do this.

THE USE OF DECEPTION IN THE JEFFERSON NEGOTIATION

Although negotiators are trained to avoid using deception in their discourse with hostage takers or other barricaded subjects, deception is a common characteristic of crisis negotiation. In fact, according to Womack and Walsh (1997), negotiators and hostage takers create "mutual deception" during a crisis incident. Sarna (1997) similarly points out that the nature of the relationship between police negotiator and hostage taker make deceptive practices between them inevitable:

> Negotiators may find themselves engaging in deception to accomplish some objective (e.g., misleading the hostage taker about a wounded person's condition). Deception by negotiators is especially risky, as it may, if detected or even suspected, undercut the formation of trust and genuineness in the police negotiator–hostage taker relationship. At worst, it can precipitate a violent response. Hence, official deception can be a risky business. Therefore, negotiators receive training in the perils of deception and countermeasures for handling discovery and the resultant threats to trust. Lying to armed, barricaded persons threatening violence is not done lightly, particularly if hostages are involved. (p. 98)

Paul talked at length about how he made sense of his decision to lie to Lewis, first about the condition of the victims and later about Lewis's likely prison sentence. Paul clearly knew that by lying, he was going against what he was trained to do as a crisis negotiator.

> The rule, "Don't lie"—don't, you know—[we] don't vary from those rules. Those were things we violated. I mean, those were cardinal rules. Don't do this. Under any circumstances . . . absolutely. Especially . . . the one that says don't lie. Because it's the one that—it was pounded in our head that that is an absolute sin to do (Paul, p. 26)

Nevertheless, Paul's training did not stop him from breaking the rule. I asked him, "What was going through your head that you decided it was time to make that decision?"

> I wouldn't call it calculated, it was one of those things that popped in my head. I said, I think it'll work. It was a gut reaction, a feeling that I'm gonna try it— if I lose, somebody else is the hero of the day; if I win, we all go home winners. And that was my premise for doing it. I felt that this was a do-or-die situation and either it's going to work and we're going to get those kids out, or it's not going to work and he'll either lose it or he'll want to talk to someone else. . . . That was the decision I made, and it wasn't much of a decision on my part; it was— I think, it was partially reaction, partially instinct and partially, I've thought about it for thirty seconds and said, What do I [have] to lose? (Paul, p. 26)

Paul was confident that he had nothing to lose. He did not think Lewis would question him, and if he did, perhaps becoming threatening or violent, Paul had a backup plan: The sniper would shoot Lewis. This information reassured Paul.

> I knew he was of no danger at this point, plus I also knew I had a sniper in place. [If] things went south, I knew, I trusted . . . that . . . the person holding the trigger wouldn't hesitate. And I knew she had him in her crosshairs, I knew if he made one wrong move, all I was going to hear was the phone drop. (Paul, p. 83)

The confidence Paul had in the sniper was the impetus behind his decision to use deception.

> I figured that I was at rock bottom at this point; I couldn't go much lower, and the worst that could happen is he'll kill somebody and we'll take him out. We were in a position to do that. Or he won't want to talk to me anymore and someone else will come in and think of another technique and I'll take a coach's role. . . . I felt that the risk far outweighed the end result if it'd been bad. (Paul, p. 26)

Paul's remarks indicate he thought only about the repercussions to Lewis or to himself. He did not consider the situation of the hostages. If Lewis had confronted Paul, the hostages might have been in immense danger. Not only would they have witnessed the sniper "taking Lewis out," but they could have been shot by Lewis, or accidentally by the sniper.

Paul had no thoughts of this until after the incident. He was later shocked that he had had so little concern about the danger he had created for the hostages:

> After I listened to [the] tape . . . it scared the hell out of me. Because I didn't give a thought to the hostages. I didn't give a thought to what could happen to them if things went south. (Paul, p. 83)

Furthermore, Paul was greatly bothered by his behavior once the shock of the incident wore off the next day:

> I felt ashamed that I would do that, knowing that people had died, you know; I beat myself up for a lot of that. I felt so horridly depressed after that. (Paul, p. 30)

At the time of the incident, Paul's disregard for the safety of the hostages was overshadowed by the momentum he felt, by what he called a "rush" to finish the job and "close the deal."

> It was an emotional roller coaster, there was no doubt about that. But I can remember—I can remember the time I was totally relaxed, I can remember the time in this thing that I felt like I was just hammering that deal home and it was—I was in the driver's seat: by God, I'm ready for him to sign! . . . It was a rush . . . beyond compare. It was a rush. . . . And I think about that real lackadaisical attitude that I had, and it was like, oh my God, what did I do? . . . in that, like, I wasn't concerned. . . . That concern wasn't there anymore, you know, the fear of somebody dying. It was, "Hammer this deal home and the hell with everybody else! ((laughs))" (Paul, p. 29)

Paul told me he felt his use of deception at Jefferson changed the rules on deception for all crisis negotiators. Prior to Jefferson, negotiators were instructed not to lie; however, after Jefferson, Paul believed, negotiators were given slightly different instruction by their trainers:

> Try not to lie. But if it's an effective tool, make sure you remember that lie, and be able to carry that lie all the way through, and if you're going to lie, you better know the dangers, you better know the risks. (Paul, p. 26)

I found the other participants who talked to me about the deception at Jefferson to be much less reflective about it. They did not doubt its utility or even its necessity. According to Don,

> it's smoke and mirrors. It has to be there. It's an invaluable element of the negotiation process. Does anyone really think in any stretch of the imagination that you can get on the phone or do a face-to-face and tell them 150 percent of the truth through the whole thing? That's absurd. You want to tell them basically what you think they need to hear, what they want to hear, what you can tell them, what you can convince them that they want to hear, or convince them of a fact whether true or not true, to benefit your position, not theirs. [Interviewer: "Which is to get them out."] Yes. You are manipulating, leading, baiting, smoke and mirrors, to do what you have to do to resolve the situation without further injury or death. That's what it comes down to. Either their injury, our injury, the neighbor's, whoever . . . you do what you have to do, you say what you have to . . . to get them out. (Don, pp. 59–60).

Bob and I also talked at length about the issue of deception. I found the following comment particularly striking:

> There are some studies—and I have read some—that say, no matter what, you never lie to them, never lie to them. Well, personally, I think that's B.S. That's my personal opinion. But I have read, by people that have done their thesis or doctor[ate] or whatever, say, This is the worst thing in the world. . . . Well, you've got eighty live bodies here. You do what you have to do. I mean, lie, the white lies that we did. There are some negotiators that say, Just don't do that. Okay. I just—I don't think *anybody* in that room—I don't think *anybody* in the room had any qualms about what we did with the letter. The chief certainly didn't, or the sheriff (Bob, p. 21).

The team's use of deception with Lewis was their way to ensure that the discourse was successful—that is, that it would end with Lewis's peaceful surrender. The team believed that for them to succeed, Lewis needed to be reassured he had not killed anyone. They suspected that he believed this already; when they lied, it was only to reaffirm his belief. Paul felt that his lies helped sustain his relationship with Lewis, as well as Lewis's relationship to himself. At the point that Paul first used deception (when he said, "No one has died"), he was concerned that Lewis was suicidal. This may have created some anxiety for the team and pressure for Paul. Although Paul was attempting to maintain the relationship by lying, he also risked the relationship by doing so.

Paul's relationship with Lewis up to the point of deception had been benevolent and sympathetic; this was evident in his language and tone of voice.

When Paul chose to lie, however, he no longer operated within these parameters. He entered a new relationship with Lewis. He addressed Lewis not from the position of a crisis negotiator trying to understand the circumstances of an emotional young man, but that of a police officer who was willing to risk Lewis's death in order to end the incident.

Managing these two conflicting relationships is the constant dilemma of the crisis negotiator. Each stance requires a different view of the person on the other end of the phone line. Each will result in a different discourse. If the hostage taker is seen only as a monster, it becomes easy to justify risking his death, which is what Paul did when he lied to Lewis. However, it is difficult to talk to a monster with genuineness and sincerity. According to crisis negotiators, the latter two qualities are required to do the work. On the other hand, if the negotiator sees the hostage taker only as a troubled person, the parameters of the relationship are similarly constrained. The negotiator may find it easy to listen to him with interest and attention; yet, this can make it more difficult to end the conversation.

In the Jefferson case, lying was a means to end the conversation. At the point Paul lied, he risked forcing the sniper to shoot Lewis, and he risked the safety of the hostages.

Paul's shift between each relationship position is evident in the discourse. The statement that "no one has died" stands apart from the rest of the conversation, for it was the first time Paul was completely dishonest. While Paul had lied about other issues, he routinely tempered his dishonesty with some version of the truth (e.g., "I'm in an office, but I couldn't tell you which one"). The contrast between his subtle and overt dishonesty is very clear. Paul's tone of voice throughout the negotiation was smooth and steady, but when he said, "No one has died," his voice changed, becoming high-pitched and broken. It is a graphic difference from the rest of Paul's conversation.

It is important to note that reflection on the negotiator's dilemma about whether or not to use deception is likely to happen in hindsight, and with an outsider's (whether it is researcher, commander, or negotiator) perspective. Further, it takes place with many comforts that negotiators do not have at the scene—time, safety, and privacy. As Sheehan, Everly, and Langlieb (2004) pointed out:

> Law enforcement professionals do not have the luxury of sitting back and theorizing when confronted with catastrophes. They usually have to act immediately to establish public order in the wake of the disorder caused by large-scale incidents. (p. 3)

A negotiator thinks, acts, and makes choices in the moment, in the midst of a media circus, and, most significantly, with the responsibility for the lives of other people. This is a very powerful charge and can overwhelm any other responsibility the negotiator might feel toward the hostage taker.

PAUL THE HERO: IMPLICATIONS FOR PRACTITIONERS OF SUCCESSFUL CRISIS NEGOTIATION

According to Vecchi (2002), "a properly handled [hostage/barricade] situation averts catastrophes and creates 'heroes'" (p. 2). In this case, Paul was indeed a hero. He received attention and accolades that eluded the rest of the team; later, his "hero" status became a source of tension when a television movie was made about the Jefferson incident, allegedly with assistance from Paul. However, Paul's special status went beyond what most people might expect; for Paul, the success of his effort resulted in mixed, ambivalent feelings about the incident and his role in it.

Theoretically, a negotiator's relationship with a hostage taker is considered temporary, null and void once the incident ends. Practically, however, I question if this is the case. In his interviews with me, Paul talked ambivalently about his feelings toward Lewis. He told me that if Lewis asked him to, he would go to visit him in prison. (He has not been asked.) He also told me that he is determined to write a book about his experience in this incident because of his promise to Lewis to tell his story. He intends the book to be for an audience of school personnel—not negotiators, not police officers. Interestingly, Paul is no longer a police officer. He left the force to become a teacher.

The other team members did not discuss with me any postincident ambivalence about their relationship with Lewis. However, several of them did acknowledge that the relationship Paul developed with Lewis on the phone is very different from what they experienced as team members. They seemed to realize that they have been able to maintain a distance from Lewis that Paul could not.

In the eyes of negotiators, a hostage taker is a person in crisis, someone who will respond to "needs fulfillment and active listening" (Vecchi, 2002, p. 2). Seeing hostage takers through this lens has consequences. Successfully building a relationship with a person in crisis (hostage taker) and genuinely appreciating his worldview can raise feelings and questions that negotiators may be unprepared for.

There is no literature about what it is like for negotiators once they have abruptly ended a successful discourse (and negotiation relationship) with a hostage taker. Interestingly, this topic is not discussed in any specific way in the crisis negotiation literature. Examination of such postincident negotiator perspectives may have important implications for negotiator training and retention and is recommended as an area of further study.

PARTICIPANTS' DESCRIPTIONS OF THE NEGOTIATION'S SUCCESS

Several team members noted reasons for the success of their effort that are unrelated to the specific communication skills discussed above. Richard felt that Lewis did not want to die and that he would have surrendered to anyone. Patricia suggested that Lewis talked to the team because he was a "virgin" at being a criminal. Bob, too, thought it would have been a very different negotiation with someone who was an "old-timer." Don, who interviewed Lewis the day after the incident, believed the negotiation worked because Lewis believed he had not killed anyone.

> He believed—he believed that we told him the absolute truth. Okay. He bought into the fact that no one had seriously hurt or killed. He believed—he truly believed that. Absolutely 150 percent. He didn't know that he killed anyone until I told him. He believed that he was going to get— I don't know why he believed it, but we all signed a letter that, we sent him a letter that, you know, we'd get minimum security, and dadadadadadadadada-da and not go to prison forever and he believed that. I don't know *why* anyone would believe that but I think he believed what he wanted to believe. . . . Even during the interview, and we're going, no, that's not true. I mean, even the next day he still bought into believing what we told him during negotiations because we were his lifeline. We were his umbilical cord. (Don, p. 59)

> I was lucky. There was no other way around it. I was just flat lucky. And the thing that saved my butt that day, the thing that solved the problem between us, was *our* mutual problems in school. Had I not done that, I wouldn't-a been any better than anybody else. (Paul, pp. 28–29)

> Paul personally was very effective. Very good. And I don't know, I think that was one of his first negotiations, too. I don't know that he had a lot of experience before, but he has that kind of personality that is real, real social, real comfortable. He was real quick to pick up on the things he needed to handle, like I mentioned the venting, initially establishing rapport, letting Lewis Johnson get it out. (Richard, p. 12)

> Seven people was a lot better than just two people. I'm sure everybody had input, everybody had something to contribute and the combination of everyone's ideas brought this to the successful conclusion that it did. (Patricia, p. 13)

We took basic, basic negotiation fundamentals, we applied them in an intelligent manner, from a group of people who brainstormed the information, a group of professional intelligent people. I mean, . . . we outbrained him is what we did, and did we do everything absolutely right? No. Okay. But we didn't do anything wrong enough to cause him to go off the deep end and start shooting at people again. Did we control the situation because of what we did? Yes. But I don't think we did anything spectacular. (Don, pp. 76–77)

I will conclude this chapter with a quote from Gary Noesner. Prior to his participation in this project, Gary had not had the opportunity to review the Jefferson negotiation tape in depth nor to analyze it in any formal way. In our IPR interview, he summarized the effectiveness of the Jefferson negotiation.

You've got this tense, volatile, situation that is very likely to end in additional violence, [the] least of which would be a suicide. But [there was] a high probability of a suicide-by-cop, [a] police officer might hurt a student—I think that's the less likely of the injuries, but it's not impossible. And yet this negotiation team, and this negotiator, basically calms the situation down, provides stability, lowers the emotional aspects of it, deescalates the confrontation, brings the subject to a point where he can more rationally consider his options and get to a point where he even believes that—that perhaps things were as not as bad as he thought and give him a spark of hope to try something, to take a chance, to trust this negotiator. It's marvelous. (Gary, p. 21)

Chapter Nine

Implications of the Study

One of the most compelling things I learned in this study was that even among law enforcement professionals, the phenomenon of crisis negotiation is not well understood. The process is often misrepresented or even overlooked by incident commanders or police media spokespersons.

At least one of the participants in this study felt that the effort made by the team in talking the hostage taker into surrendering was lost on his peers. During a press conference that Don's police department organized after the incident, a reporter asked the police spokesman, "Can you explain how Lewis Johnson surrendered?" The spokesman gave a curt and abrupt answer: "He just 'gave up.'" For Don, this comment did not do justice to the work of the team.

> We talk[ed] on the phone for seven hours, . . . [and] he agreed to come out. But what happened during those seven hours? They do not have a clue. They really don't. "They just talk[ed] to him and he agreed to come out." They have no idea of the working fundamentals of negotiations. . . . They don't know. He doesn't know. The sheriff doesn't know, she doesn't know, they don't know. And . . . I've always felt that they sold us short on this because, you know, maybe I take it personally, is they should have said, "The negotiators did this and they did an outstanding job and they worked very hard and they're trained and they're schooled and they're the experts in their craft, and if it weren't for them, we wouldn't have had it resolved like we had." (Don, p. 40)

In this study, I have tried to shed light on the expertise of law enforcement professionals called to manage a large-scale crisis—as it unfolds, in real time, and by using the one tool that too many of us take for granted: dialogue.

In conducting this study, I placed my attention on the language and conversation between people in the most fragile of circumstances, those of a life-and-death situation. My perspective is consistent with Slatkin's (2003) view of hostage incidents as crises that are really "desperate attempts" to problem-solve, "however misdirected and unconstructive" (p. 30). This study focused on how negotiators, taking a similar view toward a young man, used conversation to construct a peaceful end to solve his gravely misdirected attempt at change. In studying the communication skills used by negotiators, it is imperative that researchers make room in their methodology for comprehending the complex contextual circumstances in which these conversations occur. As Donohue (2004) stated:

> Each negotiation is a holistic event or story with a flow: external events that impact that story, characters with various orientations and goals, twists and turns in strategies, and outcomes; and it must be viewed that way—not in terms of individual strategies, frames, or styles in isolation from one another. (p. 148)

Naturalistic inquiry is characterized by a flexible and open approach to study the complex circumstances in which the discourse takes place. This open-ended approach allowed me to talk to actual negotiation practitioners about their discourse effort. Negotiators in the field have a rich tacit understanding of what they do; this study shows that there are ways for researchers to access practitioners' knowledge.

THE UTILITY OF IPR INTERVIEWS WITH NEGOTIATORS

I doubt very much I would have learned the nuances of negotiator conversation that I did had I not utilized Interpersonal Process Recall as a method. The IPR interview method is one of the most significant contributions that this study makes to the field. This method, which is typically associated with psychotherapy research and training, was similarly appropriate as a way to analyze crisis negotiation discourse research. The IPR process gave the participants a format to vividly remember, describe, and reflect on their shared experience, and it helped me experience the talk from their point of view.

The IPR compilation tape I made for participants became a vehicle through which I could "tour" the negotiation with them. As we toured, participants showed me the scenery and points of interest. They revisited the negotiation with the benefit of time, experience, and reflection. This was compelling to watch as a researcher; I think it also provided incredibly specific, beneficial data to the study.

IPR proved to be a profound method for interviewing the Jefferson crisis negotiators about the specifics of their discourse process. I suggest negotiation practitioners incorporate IPR processes into their training sequences (particularly role-plays) and that negotiation researchers, whether practitioner or academician, utilize IPR as a way to make comprehensive sense about how crisis negotiation discourse is constructed. This tool is an extremely valuable one not yet used in the field of crisis negotiation practice and research.

THE VALUE OF ETHNOGRAPHIC INTERVIEWS WITH NEGOTIATORS

The Jefferson incident was an important point in the professional lives of the participants, and for most of them, talking to me about it was the only time they had discussed it in depth. The research project gave the team an opportunity to share what they learned. They could talk about their expertise, acquired from hard experience. The Jefferson incident matured the team in a way that participating in role-plays and reading articles cannot. This research showed a discernible pattern to their successful method, a combination of learned technique and skillful improvisation.

I think the Jefferson team found it extremely beneficial to talk to me about their experience. They wanted to tell me what happened so that I could share it with other negotiators. Each team member talked about their negotiation process with familiarity, ease, curiosity, and reflection. Clearly, they valued the process of the work they did. However, it was not something they were used to discussing. One of the most valuable things this study offers to negotiators is the insight it brings about the Jefferson negotiators' process as a team. It *shows* how they worked together. It describes, from the team's point of reference, how their efforts began, developed, and coalesced into a successful result. It illustrates, in their collective voice, the incredible amount of thought, dedication, and labor they put into the process.

Ethnographic interviewing gave me a wealth of information about the context of the Jefferson crisis negotiation. An ethnographic approach helped me appreciate the incredible difficulty, complexity, and enigmatic nature of the context of the Jefferson negotiation. The ethnographic fieldwork I did helped me get a clear and strong sense of what the Jefferson team experienced. Adding ethnography to my research design had the effect of bringing the talk alive; it became richer and more vivid.

I cannot imagine this study without the input of the Jefferson team. I strongly recommend that researchers and practitioners find ways to methodically and systematically interview negotiators in the aftermath of an incident. Police agencies must learn to think about what happens beyond an incident's end, "ensuring the availability of follow-up counseling for personnel and their families, as well as others in the community" (Band & Harpold, 1999, p. 11). While negotiators often have team debriefings after an incident has ended, an in-depth interview process about the negotiation effort should take place in addition to a full team debriefing.

Fundamentally, more research with negotiators about how they do what they do is called for. Specifically, research on the actual discourse process is necessary. Additionally, the field requires more research that incorporates the views and ideas of practitioners in crisis negotiation research. Research on the negotiation process needs to actively incorporate the views of negotiators inside the research process, and researchers and practitioners would do well to focus on in-depth analysis of the communication process, from an inductive rather than deductive perspective.

Today, law enforcement officers find themselves involved in critical incidents that are "previously unthinkable situations" (Band & Harpold, 1999, p. 9). These unthinkable situations include the incidents at Columbine High School in 1999 and Virginia Polytechnic University in 2007. The effects of such shootings on our society are out of the bounds of discussion in this book; however, it is worth noting that such incidents are no longer considered exceptional. They have almost become routine. Yet we know very little about how such crises are managed in real time, from the perspectives of the professional directly involved. I hope that situation changes; we have much to learn from the people who deal with these critical incidents—and our scholarly attention to their work can yield very powerful information about what it means to resolve a crisis, when possible, through dialogue.

Jefferson was one of the first of many shooting incidents to occur in an educational setting. It is also one of the few examples we have of a police critical incident that ended successfully. That is, it ended with the hostage taker's voluntary surrender, after a long but skilled and meaningful conversation with police negotiators. Given the unpredictable and volatile nature of such critical incidents, it is imperative that law enforcement find ways to emulate the successful tactics and strategies of agencies that have dealt with similar problems (Sheehan, Everly, & Langlieb, 2004). As such, this study of the Jefferson communication effort serves as an important tool for law enforcement.

Furthermore, it should be enlightening for clinicians and researchers interested in discourse management in life-threatening situations.

The goal of this book has been to illustrate the conversational skills that worked in one successful crisis negotiation discourse. However, by incorporating the views and perspectives of the incident as well as an expert negotiator, it includes the voices of many practitioners in the field and multiple views of how a negotiation can be successful. These stories are rarely told, not because they aren't there but because it is rare to ask the questions that elicit them. In this book, I focused my attention on the stories of the Jefferson negotiators—particular to how each saw their work on that fateful day.

In the waves of grief, anger, and confusion that follow a hostage incident—particularly one at a high school—it is easy to overlook the narratives of the professionals most deeply involved in managing the crisis. Media coverage privileges stories about the perpetrator, not the police negotiators working behind the scenes. What stories do they have to tell? In this book, I provided a vivid, complex, and powerful response to that question, one that privileges the voices of the negotiators involved.

The Jefferson crisis negotiation demonstrated how a team of negotiators worked together to construct a powerful discourse effort that resulted in a peaceful ending to a deadly incident. In taking a clinical perspective toward examination of how this was achieved, I developed a research framework that utilized negotiators' expertise. This expertise needs to be tapped more often as a learning and training tool—not solely for public consumption and media exploitation but for scholarly research that can lead to in-depth understandings of critical incident management that, in turn, can inform best practices of crisis management in the future. It is my hope that further studies more actively incorporate negotiators in the same way. The microanalysis of the discourse, using the views of the negotiators who participated in it, elicited a very unique description and understanding of the crisis negotiation phenomena.

This study illustrated how negotiators used various strategies to achieve success; many of these are techniques already described in the negotiation literature. Thus, this study is an affirmation of many negotiation concepts. However, the analysis also illustrated the use of techniques not yet discussed in negotiation literature. Similarly, some of the techniques (such as how negotiators choose to repeat or ignore hostage takers' language) require further exploration and critical analysis. Such unexpected discovery reflects what Sheehan, Everly, and Langlieb (2004) noted about the benefit of exploring the process of critical incident management: "From such adversities invariably come innovations, lessons learned, and ultimately, even greater response capabilities" (p. 1). This research is a step in that direction.

References

Aston, C. (1983). Political hostage taking in Western Europe: A statistical analysis. In L. Freedman & Y. Alexander (Eds.), *Perspectives on terrorism* (pp. 99–130). Wilmington, DE: Scholarly Resources.

Band, S. R., & Harpold, J. A. (1999). School violence: Lessons learned. *FBI Law Enforcement Bulletin, 68*(9), 9–16.

Biggs, J. R. (1987). Defusing hostage situations. *Police Chief, 54*, 33–34.

Bogdan, R., & Biklen, S. (1982). *Qualitative research for education: An introduction to theory and methods*. Needham Heights, MA: Allyn & Bacon.

Bolz, F. (1981). Perspectives in hostage recovery. *Law Enforcement Communications, 9*(6), 28–29.

Boscolo, L., Cecchin, G., Hoffman, L., & Penn, P. (1987). *Milan systemic family therapy: Conversations in theory and practice*. New York: Basic.

Chenail, R. J. (1994). Qualitative research and clinical work: "Private-ization" and "Public-ation." *Qualitative Report, 2*(1). Available at http://www.nova.edu/ssss/QR/BackIssues/QR2-1/private.html.

Culley, J. (1974). Defusing human bombs: Hostage negotiations. *FBI Law Enforcement Bulletin, 43*(10), 10–14.

Dalfonzo, V. A., & Romano, S. J. (2003). Negotiation position papers: A tool for crisis negotiators. *FBI Law Enforcement Bulletin, 72*(10), 27–31.

Danto, B. L. (1979). New frontiers in the relationship between suicidology and law enforcement. *Suicide and Life-Threatening Behavior, 9*(4), 195–204.

DiVasto, P. [V.], Lanceley, F. J., & Gruys, A. (1992). Critical issues in suicide intervention. *FBI Law Enforcement Bulletin, 61*(8), 13–16.

DiVasto, P. V., & Newman, S. L. (1993, May). The four C's of hostage negotiation. *Law and Order*, 82–87.

Donohue, W. A. (2004). Critical moments as "flow" in negotiation. *Negotiation Journal*, 147–51.

Donohue, W. A., & Ramesh, C. N. (1992). Negotiator–opponent relationships. In L. L. Putnam & M. E. Roloff (Eds.), *Communication and Negotiation* (pp. 209–32). Newbury Park, CA: Sage.

Donohue, W. A., Ramesh, C. [N.], & Borchgrevink, C. (1991). Crisis bargaining: Tracking relational paradox in hostage negotiation. *International Journal of Conflict Management, 2*(4), 257–274.

Donohue, W. A., Ramesh, C. [N.], Kaufmann, G., & Smith, R. (1991). Crisis bargaining in intense conflict situations. *International Journal of Group Tensions, 21*(2), 133–53.

Donohue, W. A., & Roberto, A. J. (1993). Relational development as negotiated order in hostage negotiation. *Human Communication Research, 20*(2), 175–198.

Elliott, R. (1986). Interpersonal Process Recall (IPR) as a psychotherapy process research method. In L. S. Greenberg & W. Pinsof (Eds.), *The psychotherapeutic process: A research handbook* (pp. 503–27). New York: Guilford Press.

Everstine, D. S., Bodin, A. M., & Everstine, L. (1977). Emergency psychology: A mobile service for police crisis calls. *Family Process, 16*(3), 281–92.

Feldmann, T. B., & Johnson, P. W. (1995). Psychotherapeutic and self psychology principles to hostage negotiations. *Journal of the American Academy of Psychoanalysis, 23*(2), 207–21.

Fetterman, D. (1989). *Ethnography: Step by Step*. Newbury Park, CA: Sage.

Friedland, N., & Merari, A. (1992). Hostage events: Descriptive profile and analysis of outcomes. *Journal of Applied Social Psychology, 22*(2), 134–156.

Fuselier, G. D. (1988). Hostage negotiation consultant: Emerging role for the clinical psychologist. *Professional Psychology: Research and Practice, 19*(2), 175–79.

Fuselier, G. W. (1981a). A practical overview of hostage negotiations (part 1). *FBI Law Enforcement Bulletin, 50*(6), 2–6.

Fuselier, G. W. (1981b). A practical overview of hostage negotiations (conclusion). *FBI Law Enforcement Bulletin, 50*(7), 10–15.

Gale, J., Odell, M., & Nagireddy, C. (1995). Marital therapy and self-reflexive research: Research and/as intervention. In G. H. Morris & R. J. Chenail (Eds.), *The talk of the clinic: Explorations in the analysis of medical and therapeutic discourse* (pp. 105–29). Hillsdale, NJ: Lawrence Erlbaum Associates.

Geertz, C. (1973). *The Interpretation of Cultures*. New York: Basic.

Gist, R. M., & Perry, J. D. (1985). Perspectives on negotiation in local jurisdictions, part 1: A different typology of situations. *FBI Law Enforcement Bulletin, 54*(11), 21–24.

Goldaber, I. (1979). A typology of hostage-takers. *Police Chief, 46*(6), 21–23.

Hammer, M. R., Van Zandt, C. R., & Rogan, R. G. (1994). Crisis/hostage negotiation team profile. *FBI Law Enforcement Bulletin, 63*(3), 8–11.

Hassel, C. V. (1975). The hostage situation: Exploring the motivation and the cause. *Police Chief, 42*(9), 55–58.

Heyman, P. B. (1993). *Lessons of Waco: Proposed changes in federal law enforcement*. Report to the deputy attorney general on the events at Waco, Texas, February 28–April 19, 1993. Washington, DC: U.S. Department of Justice.

Johnson, T. A. (1978). A role for the behavioral scientist in hostage negotiation incidents. *Journal of Forensic Sciences, 23*(4), 797–803.
Kagan, N. I., & Kagan, H. (1990). IPR: A validated model for the 1990s and beyond. *Counseling Psychologist, 18*(3), 436–440.
Kraus, S., Wilkenfeld, J., Harris, M. A., & Blake, E. (1992). The hostage crisis simulation. *Simulation & Gaming, 23*(4), 398–416.
Lincoln, Y., & Guba, E. (1985). *Naturalistic Inquiry*. Newbury Park, CA: Sage.
Maher, G. F. (1977). *Hostage: A police approach to a contemporary crisis*. Springfield, IL: Charles C. Thomas.
McMains, M. J., & Mullins, W. C. (1996). *Crisis negotiations: Managing critical incidents and hostage situations in law enforcement and corrections*. Cincinnati, OH: Anderson.
Miller, A. (1979). Hostage negotiations and the concept of transference. In Y. Alexander, D. Carlton, & P. Wilkinson (Eds.), *Terrorism: Theory and practice* (pp. 137–58). Boulder, CO: Westview Press.
Moerman, M. (1988). *Talking culture: Ethnography and conversation analysis*. Philadelphia: University of Pennsylvania Press.
Morse, J. (1994). "Emerging from the data": The cognitive processes of analysis in qualitative inquiry. In J. M. Morse (Ed.), *Critical issues in qualitative research methods* (pp. 23–43). Thousand Oaks, CA: Sage.
Noesner, G. W., & Dolan, J. T. (1992). First responder negotiation training. *FBI Law Enforcement Bulletin, 61*(8), 1–4.
Noesner, G. W., & Webster, M. (1997). Crisis intervention: Using active listening skills in negotiations. *FBI Law Enforcement Bulletin, 66*(8), 13–19.
Potter, J., & Wetherell, M. (1987). *Discourse and social psychology: Beyond attitudes and behavior*. Beverly Hills, CA: Sage.
Regini, C. (2002). Crisis negotiation teams: Selection and training. *FBI Law Enforcement Bulletin, 71*(11), 1–5.
Regini, C. (2004). Crisis intervention for law enforcement negotiators. *FBI Law Enforcement Bulletin, 73*(10), 1–6.
Reiser, M., & Sloane, M. (1983). The use of suggestibility techniques in hostage negotiation. In L. Z. Freedman & Y. Alexander (Eds.), *Perspectives on terrorism* (pp. 213–23). Wilmington, DE: Scholarly Resources.
Rodriguez, G. J., & Franklin, D. (1986). Training hostage negotiators with psychiatric patients: A "hands-on" approach. In J. T. Reese & H. A. Goldstein (Eds.), *Psychological services for law enforcement* (pp. 497–500). Washington, DC: GPO.
Rogan, R. G., & Hammer, M. R. (1994). Crisis negotiations: A preliminary investigation of facework in naturalistic conflict discourse. *Journal of Applied Communication Research, 22*, 216–231.
Sarna, P. (1997). Models for managing hostage negotiations: Pathways or straitjackets? In R. G. Rogan, M. R. Hammer, & C. R. Van Zandt (Eds.), *Dynamic processes of crisis negotiation: Theory, research, and practice* (pp. 95–103). Westport, CT: Praeger.
Schenkein, J. (1978). *Studies in the organization of conversational interaction*. New York: Academic Press.

Schlossberg, H. (1979). Police response to hostage situations. In J. T. O'Brien & M. Marcus (Eds.), *Crime and justice in America: Critical issues for the future* (pp. 209–20). New York: Pergamon Press.

Schlossberg, H., & Freeman, L. (1974). *Psychologist with a gun*. New York: Cowan, McCann & Geoghegan.

Sheehan, D. C., Everly, G. S., & Langlieb, A. (2004). Current best practices: Coping with major critical incidents. *FBI Law Enforcement Bulletin, 73*(9), 1–13.

Slatkin, A. (2003). Suicide risk and hostage/barricade situations involving older persons. *FBI Law Enforcement Bulletin, 72*(4), 26–31.

Soskis, D. A. (1983). Behavioral scientists and law enforcement personnel: Working together on the problem of terrorism. *Behavioral Sciences & the Law, 1*(2), 47–58.

Spradley, J. P. (1979). *The ethnographic interview*. New York: Holt, Rinehart & Winston.

Tannen, D. (Ed). (1989). *Talking voices: Repetition, dialogue, and imaging in conversational discourse*. Cambridge: Cambridge University Press.

Taylor, S. J., & Bogdan, R. (1984). *Introduction to qualitative research methods: The search for meanings* (2nd ed.). New York: John Wiley & Sons.

Terhune-Bickler. (2004). Too close for comfort: Negotiating with fellow officers. *FBI Law Enforcement Bulletin, 73*(4), 1–5.

Vecchi, G. M. (2002). Hostage/barricade management. *FBI Law Enforcement Bulletin (71)*5, 1–7.

Weiss, R. S. (1994). *Learning from strangers: The art and method of qualitative interview studies*. New York: Free Press.

Welch, M. F. (1984). The applied typology and victimology in the hostage negotiation process. *Crime and Justice, 7,* 63–86.

Wind, B. A. (1995). Guide to crisis negotiations. *FBI Law Enforcement Bulletin, 64*(10), 7–11.

Womack, D. F., & Walsh, K. (1997). A three-dimensional model of relationship development in hostage negotiations. In R. G. Rogan, M. R. Hammer, & C. R. Van Zandt (Eds.), *Dynamic processes of crisis negotiation: Theory, research, and practice* (pp. 57–75). Westport, CT: Praeger.

Index

1st moment: 4:25 P.M.:
  arrival of negotiators, 33–34;
  bathroom keys, 41, 43;
  conversations with Alan, 34–36;
  discussion of "bad raps," 44;
  discussion of prison, 43–44;
  end of call, 57–58;
  Lewis agrees to negotiate, 48–49;
  Lewis asks about outside surroundings, 47–48;
  Lewis asks for news reporter, 57;
  Lewis asks Paul's location, 54–55;
  Lewis asks Paul to call back, 54;
  Lewis calms down, 45–46;
  Lewis discusses failing grade, 37–39;
  Lewis needs time to think, 53–54;
  name of hostage taker, 41–42;
  pattern of teamwork, 49–50;
  Paul becomes liaison, 46–47;
  Paul discusses Mr. Grant, 52–53;
  Paul feels personal connection to Lewis, 51–52;
  Paul's focus on present, 44–45;
  Paul's self-disclosure, 50–51;
  Paul's status, 36–37;
  request for news reporter, 39–40;
  softening of language, 40–41

2nd moment: 6:00 P.M.:
  Alan fields call for Lewis, 59;
  change in negotiators, 59–62;
  Lewis asks to speak with Paul, 65–66;
  Richard introduces himself to Lewis, 62–63;
  Richard suggests that Lewis release some hostages, 64

3rd moment: 6:15 P.M.:
  advice from Van Zandt, 84–85;
  checking status of victims, 76–77;
  FBI provides psychological profile, 84;
  key events before 8:30, 86;
  Lewis discusses comfort level in building, 70–72;
  Lewis discusses future options, 83–84;
  Lewis discusses prison sentence, 73–74;
  Lewis minimizes behavior, 74–75;
  Lewis requests aspirin, 81–82;
  Lewis requests reporters, 79–81;
  Lewis requests television, 77–78;
  Paul affirms Lewis's importance, 81;
  Paul compliments Lewis, 77;
  Paul discusses ending incident, 78–79;

134 Index

Paul discusses Lewis's
  trustworthiness, 82–83;
Paul speaks with Alan, 67–68;
Paul speaks with Lewis about
  Richard, 69;
Paul suggests that Lewis come out, 73;
SWAT officer enters building, 69–70;
withholding of information from
  Lewis, 75–76
4th moment: 8:30 P.M.:
  discussion of Ms. Munroe, 93;
  discussion of seriousness of crimes,
    94–95;
  Lewis discusses school experience,
    88–89;
  Lewis reveals about letter, 92;
  Lewis's parents, 90–91;
  offer of tape recorder, 87–88;
  Paul asks about Nathan, 91–92;
  Paul discusses ending of incident,
    95–96;
  Paul discusses prison time, 96
5th moment: 9:40 P.M.:
  end of incident, 102–103;
  Lewis surrenders, 101–102;
  Paul discusses Lewis's "bad rap,"
    99–100;
  Paul discusses prison sentence and
    condition of victims, 97–99;
  Paul discusses surrender, 100–101;
  written terms of surrender, 101

Alan (hostage), 34–36, 59, 65, 67–68
archive, FBI, 12
aspirin, request for, 81–82
audiotapes, 12, 19
audit trails, 25–26

"bad raps," 44
Bob (negotiator):
  1st moment: 4:25 P.M.:
    arrival of, 34;
    on failing grade, 38;
    on Lewis's agreement to
      negotiate, 49;
    on pattern of teamwork, 49;
    on timing of Paul's callback, 56;
  **2nd–5th moments: 6:00 P.M.–9:40
    P.M.:**
    arrival of, 60–61;
    on control of information, 76;
    on Lewis's readiness to give up,
      91;
    on Van Zandt's predictions, 85;
    on written terms of surrender,
      101;
    on deception, 117;
    on lack of interference, 107;
    role in negotiation, 20 (table),
      22–23

case study approach, 11
change in negotiators, 59–62, 107
clues, fishing for, 109–10
collaborative atmosphere, 107
Columbine High School, 126
commitments, forming, 111
communication skills, 10
confidentiality, 18
confirmability, 25–26
consultant, Paul as, 110
conversation:
  staying in, 109;
  value of, 2–3, 123–24
credibility, 26–27
crisis incidents, types of, 8
crisis negotiation:
  defined, 5, 7;
  elements of success, 106–108,
    120–21;
  history of, 7–8;
  patterns of effective, 108–12;
  patterns of ineffective, 112–14;
  preparatory study of, 18–19;
  skills needed for, 8–9;
  tasks performed in, 9–10

data analysis:
  approach to, 27–28;
  step 1: transcription, 27–28;

step 2: combining transcript and
  interview data, 29–30;
step 3: creating a narrative, 30–31
data collection:
  fieldwork interviews, 19–20;
  preparation for, 18–19;
  site visits, 23–24
deception, 95, 97–98, 114–19
dependability, 26
disarming via conversation, 3, 6n2
discourse analysis, 15
Dog Day Afternoon (motion picture), 19
domestic disputes, 8
Don (negotiator):
  arrives on scene, 33–34;
  on Lewis's intelligence level, 54;
  on pattern of teamwork, 50;
  on control of information, 75–76;
  on deception, 117;
  on isolation of team, 106;
  on peers' perceptions of incident, 123;
  on reasons for success, 120–21;
  role in negotiation, 20 (table), 21–22

Ellen (negotiator):
  arrives on scene, 34;
  on checking status of victims, 77;
  on end of incident, 102;
  on Lewis's request to speak with Paul, 66;
  role in negotiation, 20 (table), 21;
  on timing of Paul's callback, 56
ethnographic interviewing, 15–17, 125–26

FBI Law Enforcement Bulletin, 19
Federal Bureau of Investigation (FBI):
  adoption of negotiation strategies, 8;
  assistance with preliminary research, 18–19;
  local team's perceptions of, 61–62;
  tape archive held by, 12
flexibility, 107

Grant (teacher), 1, 33, 37
group interviews, 13–14

helper, Paul as, 37, 110
hero, Paul as, 119
hooks, 10, 37, 109–10
hostage crises, as type of crisis incident, 8
hostage negotiation (term), 7
hypnotic suggestion techniques, 10

information, control of, 75–76
interference, lack of, 106–107
Interpersonal Process Recall (IPR), 17, 19, 124–25
interrupting, 114
interviews:
  combining with transcript, 29–30;
  decision to conduct, 13;
  ethnographic, 15–17, 125–26;
  protocol used for, 13–14
IPR. *See* Interpersonal Process Recall
isolation of team, 106
"I understand," saying, 113

Jane (negotiator):
  1st moment: 4:25 P.M.:
    arrives on scene, 34;
    on failing grade, 38;
    on Lewis's need for time to think, 53–54;
    notes that Lewis has calmed down, 46;
    on pattern of teamwork, 50;
  2nd moment: 6:00 P.M.:
    on arrival of FBI, 60–61;
    on change in negotiators, 60;
    on Lewis's request to speak with Paul, 65, 66;
  3rd–5th moments: 6:15 p.m.–9:40 P.M.:
    on control of information, 76;
    on end of incident, 102;
    on Lewis's acknowledgment of seriousness of crimes, 94;

interview of, 23;
role in negotiation, 20–21, 20 (table);
on suspension of time, 106
Johnson, Lewis. *See* Lewis

keys, bathroom, 41, 43

language, use of hostage taker's, 112
legal mandate, 8
Leo (hostage taker). *See* Lewis
letter left by Lewis, 92
Lewis (hostage taker):
  1st moment: 4:25 P.M.:
    agrees to negotiate, 48–49;
    asks about outside surroundings, 47–48;
    asks for news reporter, 57;
    asks Paul's location, 54–55;
    asks Paul to call back, 54–56;
    calms down, 45–46;
    discusses "bad raps," 44;
    discusses failing grade, 37–39;
    discusses Paul's status, 36–37;
    discusses tricks, 40;
    ends call, 57–58;
    needs time to think, 53–54;
    provides name, 41–42;
    requests news reporter, 39–40;
    softening of language, 40–41;
  2nd moment: 6:00 P.M., 62–64;
  3rd moment: 6:15 P.M.:
    on comfort level in building, 70–72;
    discusses future options, 83–84;
    discusses prison sentence, 73–74;
    doesn't check status of victims, 76–77;
    expresses trust for Paul, 82–83;
    minimizes behavior, 74–75;
    releases hostages, 67;
    requests aspirin, 81–82;
    requests reporters, 79–81;
    requests television, 77–78;
    speaks to Paul about Richard, 69;

  4th moment: 8:30 P.M.:
    acknowledges seriousness of crimes, 94–95;
    discusses Ms. Munroe, 93;
    discusses Nathan, 91–92;
    discusses parents, 90–91;
    discusses school experience, 88–89;
    refuses offer of tape recorder, 87–88;
    reveals about letter, 92;
  5th moment: 9:40 P.M.:
    discusses "bad rap," 99–100;
    discusses prison sentence and condition of victims, 97–99;
    requests written terms of surrender, 101;
    surrenders, 101–102;
    exclusion from study, 105
library research, 23–24
limitations of study, 105
listening, active, 10, 108
lying, 95, 97–98, 114–19

"manna from Heaven," 108–109
markers, conversational, 113–14
media, news, 10
minimization, 74–75
Munroe (teacher), 1, 93, 109

narrative creation, 30–31
naturalistic inquiry, 12
negotiators:
  roles of, in Jefferson incident, 20–23, 20 (table);
  skills needed by, 8–9;
  tasks performed by, 9–10
news media, 10
New York Police Department (NYPD), 8
Noesner, Gary:
  1st moment: 4:25 P.M.:
    on Lewis's agreement to negotiate, 49;
    on Lewis's self-disclosure, 51;

Index

on Paul's personal connection to Lewis, 52;
on Paul's use of Lewis's name, 56–57;
on timing of Paul's callback, 55;
2nd–4th moments: 6:00 P.M.–8:30 P.M.:
on change in negotiators, 60;
on Lewis's minimization, 75;
on Lewis's solicitude for students, 82;
on necessity of lying, 95;
on Paul's complimenting of Lewis, 77;
on Paul's inquiry concerning hostages, 68;
on Paul's suggestion that Lewis come out, 73;
on Paul's suggestion to end incident, 79;
assistance with preliminary research, 19;
assistance with tape selection, 18;
on contributions of Paul, 108;
expertise of, 3;
interview of, 24;
on reasons for success, 121
notation legend, 29 (table)

overview of Jefferson incident, 4

paradigm shifts, 9
parallel methodological approach, 28
Patricia (negotiator):
1st moment: 4:25 P.M.:
arrives on scene, 34;
on Lewis's readiness to talk, 50–51;
on pattern of teamwork, 50;
5th moment: 9:40 P.M.:
on end of incident, 102–103;
on written terms of surrender, 101;
initial meeting with, 13;

on Lewis's request to speak with Paul, 65–66;
on reasons for success, 120;
role in negotiation, 20 (table), 21–22;
on suspension of time, 106
Paul (negotiator):
1st moment: 4:25 P.M.:
arranges to call Lewis back, 54–56;
arrives on scene, 34;
asks for name, 41–42;
calms Lewis down, 45–46;
conversations with Alan, 34–36;
discusses "bad raps," 44;
discusses failing grade, 37–39;
discusses his location, 54–55;
discusses Mr. Grant, 52–53;
discusses prison, 43–44;
discusses status, 36–37;
ends call, 57–58;
explains about keys, 43;
feels personal connection to Lewis, 51–52;
focus on present, 44–45;
on Lewis's need for time to think, 54;
as liaison, 46–47, 56;
offers to negotiate, 48–49;
responds to question about outside surroundings, 47–48;
self-disclosure by, 50–51;
softening of language by, 40–41;
2nd moment: 6:00 P.M.:
on arrival of FBI, 60;
on effect of SWAT team rescue, 65, 66;
on SWAT team rescue, 62;
3rd moment: 6:15 P.M.:
affirms Lewis's importance, 81;
on comfort level in building, 70–72;
compliments Lewis, 77;
on control of information, 76;
discusses ending incident, 78–79;

discusses Lewis's future options, 83–84;
discusses Lewis's trustworthiness, 82–83;
discusses prison sentence, 73–74;
exchange with Alan, 67–68;
expresses confidence, 68–69;
on Lewis's request for television, 77–78;
on psychological profile, 84;
responds to Lewis's request for reporters, 79–81;
suggests that Lewis come out, 73;
4th moment: 8:30 P.M.:
asks about Nathan, 91–92;
concerns about suicidality, 92–93;
discusses ending of incident, 95–96;
discusses letter, 92;
discusses Lewis's parents, 90–91;
discusses Lewis's school experience, 88–89;
discusses Ms. Munroe, 93;
discusses prison time, 96;
discusses victims' injuries, 94–95;
on necessity of lying, 95;
offers tape recorder, 87–88;
sincerity of, 89–90;
5th moment: 9:40 P.M.:
discusses Lewis's "bad rap," 99–100;
discusses prison sentence and condition of victims, 97–99;
discusses surrender, 100–101;
provides written terms of surrender, 101;
contributions of, 107–108;
on deception, 115–16;
postincident repercussions, 119–20;
on reasons for success, 120;
role in negotiation, 20–21, 20 (table)
peers' perceptions of incident, 123

permission, asking, 111
perspective, hostage taker's, 9–10
"planting seeds," 110–11
police officials, 10
postincident repercussions, 119–20
premature resolution, attempts at, 113
present, focus on, 44–45
press releases, 76
profile, psychological, 84–86

qualitative research:
approach to data analysis, 27–28;
interview process and, 13–14;
trustworthiness of, 25–27
questions, research, 11

raw data, 25–26
relevance of data, 30
reporters, news, 10
Richard (negotiator):
arrival of, 34, 60–61;
introduces himself to Lewis, 62–63;
on Lewis's request to speak with Paul, 66;
suggests that Lewis release some hostages, 64;
on reasons for success, 120
role in negotiation, 20 (table), 22–23

Schlossberg, Harvey, 8
site visits, 23–24
softening of language, 40–41, 112
staying in conversation, 109
suicidality, concerns about, 92–93
suicide attempts, 8
SWAT officers:
aligning with, 113;
arrive on scene, 33–34;
effect on negotiation process, 10;
enter building, 69–70;
rescue students on first floor, 62, 65
switching, 111–12

Taft, Nathan, 91–92
tape recorder, offer of, 87–88

television, request for, 77–78
television reporters, 10
textbook example, Jefferson incident as, 5
time, suspension of, 106
transcription, data, 28–29

transferability, 27
trustworthiness of research, 25–27

value judgments, 10
Van Zandt, Clint, 84–85
Virginia Polytechnic University, 2, 126

About the Author

Laurie L. Charlés is an assistant professor of family therapy at the University of Massachusetts, Boston. She is the author of *Intimate Colonialism: Head, Heart, and Body in West African Development Work*, a memoir of her tour in the U.S. Peace Corps (Togo, 1999–2001). Dr. Charlés's current crisis intervention research focuses on the experiences of refugees and survivors of war and political torture, particularly the experience of women and young girls. Her publications have appeared in *The Journal of Systemic Therapy*, *The Journal of Marital Family Therapy*, *Qualitative Inquiry*, *Hispanic Outlook in Higher Education*, and the *Boston Globe Magazine*.